CLOSING THE ATTAINMENT GAP IN SCHOOLS

Closing the Attainment Gap in Schools explores the experience and history of teachers who have a determined, no-nonsense approach to providing an excellent standard of education to all young people from differing backgrounds. Using professional conversations, voices are given to schools and teachers striving successfully to address this important issue through evidence-based practices. Linked with the Ad Astra Primary Partnership, what these teachers do with their schoolchildren will resonate with all schools in any location.

From Superstar Assemblies to encourage their dreams and aspirations; to Munch 'n Mingle sessions to encourage healthy eating; to Marvellous Me software to encourage the use of open-ended questions and parent–child conversations at home; and through to the use of skilled specialists to develop their handwriting skills, this book:

- explores the rich complexity of teacher learning;
- contains numerous case studies and examples of success;
- reflects upon and considers evidence-based pedagogy, practical wisdom, teacher-research, self-improving school systems and social justice;
- proposes a rich array of approaches and suggests ways forward.

Offering first-hand, invaluable and practical advice this wide-ranging book will encourage and enable any teacher to develop their own practical wisdom and a 'can do' approach whilst never shying away from the very real issues within education.

Antony Luby has been a Chartered Teacher and senior lecturer for over 40 years. His research and scholarship has mostly been based on classroom teaching i.e. MPhil, MTh, MSc and PhD and his publications address a wide range of audiences from fellow teachers in the education press (e.g. *Times Educational Supplement Scotland*) fellow practitioners in professional journals (e.g. the College of Teachers' *Education Today* and the Chartered College of Teaching's *Impact*) and fellow academics (e.g. *Educational Action Research, Quality Assurance in Education*).

CLOSING THE ATTAINMENT GAP IN SCHOOLS

Progress through Evidence-based Practices

Antony Luby

Routledge
Taylor & Francis Group

LONDON AND NEW YORK

First published 2021
by Routledge
2 Park Square, Milton Park, Abingdon, Oxon OX14 4RN

and by Routledge
52 Vanderbilt Avenue, New York, NY 10017

Routledge is an imprint of the Taylor & Francis Group, an informa business

© 2021 Antony Luby

British Library Cataloguing-in-Publication Data
A catalogue record for this book is available from the British Library

Library of Congress Cataloging-in-Publication Data
Names: Luby, Antony, author.
Title: Closing the attainment gap in schools: progress
through evidence-based practices / Antony Luby.
Description: Abingdon, Oxon; New York, NY: Routledge, 2020. |
Includes bibliographical references and index.
Identifiers: LCCN 2020014171 | ISBN 9780367344870 (hardback) |
ISBN 9780367344900 (paperback) | ISBN 9780429326165 (ebook)
Subjects: LCSH: Academic achievement–Great Britain. |
Educational attainment–Great Britain.
Classification: LCC LB1062.6 .L84 2020 | DDC 371.26/40941–dc23
LC record available at https://lccn.loc.gov/2020014171

ISBN: 978-0-367-34487-0 (hbk)
ISBN: 978-0-367-34490-0 (pbk)
ISBN: 978-0-429-32616-5 (ebk)

Typeset in Interstate
by Newgen Publishing UK

CONTENTS

FOREWORD

Professional learning that inspires great teaching

This wide-ranging book explores, often through detailed first-hand professional conversations, the experience and history of teachers engaged in their own learning as they seek to address the attainment gap. Alongside these individual stories we hear repeatedly of the importance of team and of the collective. Our author draws upon his life experiences to remind us of cyclical development, the risks of seeking to find 'what works' and the folly of forgetting the old in our haste to invent the new. Any tendency towards cynicism, however, is countered by the perpetual optimism and energy of the great teachers that Luby shares with us via extracts of dialogue. We hear the voice of brilliant teachers and their passion cannot fail to impress.

As a teacher myself, and subsequently as headteacher for 14 years, engagement with the research process as an insider-researcher for *Creating Learning without Limits* (Swann et al., 2012) was a truly transformative experience. Looking back, I realise that pleasing external inspectors was obviously important but nowhere near as vital as staying true to my values and beliefs under the scrutiny of academic researchers. This meant that the vision for creating a 'centre of excellence' for both children and teachers began to come to fruition and exceeded the judgement criteria of inspection teams when they came to call. As we documented the journey of an alternative approach to school improvement I realised how professional knowledge, growth and the learning of every child and teacher as a collective endeavour was something that I could help others to embrace. Although I didn't know this at the time, we were participating in a form of *Leerkracht* as described in Chapter 6. Every member of staff almost without exception was engaged in the process of professional development and learning. Four teaching assistants studied for a degree with three of them subsequently becoming teachers. Others studied for further degrees or engaged in programmes such as Maths Mastery or Therapeutic Specialism. The school as a teaching school, worked with hundreds of teachers sharing examples of both student and teacher agency through curriculum design and formative assessment. Throughout our school community we sought to offer joyful experiences that built a culture of can-do, all the while refusing to take a deterministic attitude, or to label by so-called 'ability'.

It is this relentless hope for a better future that forms the bedrock of the Chartered College of Teaching, established in England in 2017. The notion of connecting, supporting and celebrating teachers as professionals underpins all of our work as we develop career pathways and endeavour to make research findings accessible and useful in classrooms.

The establishment of the College comes at a time when England has a wealth of initiatives aimed at improving education through lessons from research. We are told in these pages of a range of developments and although our author cannot help but look at the emerging Chartered College of Teaching through his own experience as a Scottish Chartered Teacher there is much to encourage us as we try to embrace collegiality, this time through voluntary mass membership. In Chapter 8 we hear from a teacher from the first cohort of *CTeach* who gives us an impressive insight into the ways she is using her own learning to support others throughout her Trust. We too are seeking to build a community from the bottom-up and our new financial independence from the British Government is an encouraging sign of genuine teacher community.

Teachers need to be encouraged to develop their intuitive skills alongside learning more about pedagogy, educational research, curriculum design and assessment. This book explores the rich complexity of teacher learning whilst never shying away from the very real issues in education, such as poverty. As a teacher in the classroom I knew that the job was never finished. Never did I leave school at the end of a day, a week, a term, believing that everything had been completed. What was necessary was to make sure as far as possible, that the important things had been achieved. The same is true for professional learning. We will never truly find the answer because the problem is too intricate, multifaceted and demanding. We can, however, recognise the truth of the importance of collaboration and kindness. This book offers a rich array of approaches and suggests some ways forward. Open your mind, enjoy the privilege of listening-in to a wide variety of professional conversations and allow yourself to reflect on your own successes. Teaching is never easy, but to teach is to learn. We know that the children who need us most, thrive when they have an excellent teacher. What greater imperative could there possibly be to develop evidence-informed practice?

Professor Dame Alison Peacock
Chief Executive
The Chartered College of Teaching
www.chartered.college

Reference

Swann, M., Peacock, A., Hart, S. and Drummond, M. J. 2012. *Creating Learning without Limits*. Maidenhead: Open University Press.

1 Forging ahead in the East Midlands

Mansfield no more
Newark no more
Worksop no more
    (Luby 2019:8)

The plaintive cry from The Proclaimers 'mourning over the devastation wreaked upon Bathgate, Linwood and Methil in the industrial heartlands of their native Scotland' (Luby, 2019: 8) in *Letter from America* is adapted for the sorrow that has been poured out for the former mining towns and villages of Nottinghamshire. In the last few years I have been humbled to witness the inspiring efforts of dedicated primary school staff alleviating the poverty wrought upon the children of these towns and villages. And it all began with a chance conversation.

That chance arose in a nondescript seminar room of the cathedral city of Lincoln's Bishop Grosseteste University. However, nondescript is not a word to be used for my partner in conversation – Lee Hessey, Executive Principal of The Forge Trust comprising seven schools in the East Midlands. *A diamond in the rough* is a more apt description for Lee. Physically imposing, he shares the same characteristics of honesty and humility lauded by Sir Steve Lancashire (2019) in his review of Steve Munby's (2019) book *Imperfect Leadership*. Notably, though, neither Lee nor The Forge Trust come alone. Born of similar stock is Grant Worthington, formerly head teacher of Forest View Junior School and now a member of Quality Assurance and School Improvement with the Flying High Trust. Down-to-earth is another of the attributes that they share as exemplified by their conversation whilst surveying the football field of a struggling primary school that no-one wants – except them:

GRANT: How many is that then?
LEE: I make it four.
GRANT: So, that's four syringes on the football field. What about the dog poo?
LEE: Let's not go there...!

                              (Luby and Beckley 2019)

Others see failure and waste; but Grant and Lee see opportunity and challenge. For Grant, it is an opportunity to revive the fortunes of his old primary school; whilst for Lee it is the challenge of growing The Forge Trust.

The Ad Astra Primary Partnership

In early 2015, Lee introduced me to fellow members of the Ad Astra Primary Partnership which, at that time, comprised six Nottinghamshire schools – one primary academy, three primary schools, one junior school and one infant school. They shared the challenge and also their expertise of narrowing the attainment gap for white working class pupils sited in areas of deprivation.

The Ad Astra member schools:

- Lee at The Sir Donald Bailey Academy, Newark that, according to the Index of Multiple Deprivation is sited within the top 6% most deprived neighbourhoods.
- Grant at Forest View Junior School in New Ollerton that is situated close to Newark and Sherwood 001A within the top 10% most deprived areas.
- Head teacher Helen Chambers of Abbey Hill Primary and Nursery School sited five miles south-west of the town of Mansfield and serving an area of high social and economic disadvantage as attested by 47% of the pupils living in families that are income deprived. The school receives substantial pupil premium funding and a significant number of families are supported by social services with the school employing a full-time Child and Family Support Worker.
- Head teacher (and now Her Majesty's Inspector (HMI)) Peter Stonier then at Jacksdale Primary and Nursery School that is close to the Derbyshire border. Situated within the heart of Jacksdale village, there are 250 pupils on the school roll including a number of children from Amber Valley which is in the top 10% most deprived areas nationally.
- Head teacher Chris Wilson of Ramsden primary school in the deceptively picturesque Carlton-in-Lindrick near Worksop. The housing scheme from which the majority of pupils are drawn is found in Bassetlaw 004A that according to the Index of Multiple Deprivation is also in the top 10% of England's most deprived areas.
- And last, but not least, Jo Cook at Hallcroft Infant School that is sited not far from Bassetlaw 008A within the top 20% most deprived areas nationally.[1]

The Ad Astra Primary Partnership focuses on significant factors affecting outcomes for pupils in areas of deprivation, namely:

- material poverty;
- emotional poverty;
- poverty of experience;
- poverty of language; and
- poverty of aspiration.

The group investigates strategies and ideas for minimising the impact of such poverty on their children and the approach of the Ad Astra Primary Partnership is one of collaboration between equal partners, working in similar contexts, but with one shared ambition to identify and implement the most effective strategies to address this long-standing issue. The partnership schools are also responsive to the assertion by Hammersley-Fletcher et al. (2015:5) that:

> The strengths of schools working alongside researchers ... is an effective and supportive way to develop practices which are led and informed by schools themselves, bringing

them an extra level of autonomy to pursue issues and change initiatives that are relevant to their own setting and context.

This is evidenced by their openness to a series of research consultancy projects (Luby, 2016b) that culminates with five-day ethnographic studies in five of the partnership schools (Puttick et al., 2020).

The nitty-gritty of what some of the Ad Astra partnership schools actually do in the classroom to address poverty will be discussed later; but, for now, let us focus on the professional conversation with Lee.[2]

Thursday, 2 May 2019
The Forge Trust centre, North Muskham, Notts

AL: I'm with Lee Hessey who is the Chief Executive Officer of The Forge Trust and Lee we're discussing leadership. Would you like to just tell me what's your ... where did it all start for you?

LEE: Yeah, I started as a young teacher who came into teaching from business, so always had a view of teaching possibly different to the majority of teachers because I didn't go from school to school; I went from school at 16 to work for Wilkinson's at the time and then a couple of years later, Unilever in the big wide world. I went and got my qualifications at night school. So I wasn't your typical orthodox route, it was very unorthodox which is probably why some of my views are probably really challenging for the profession because I have views that aren't in line with the profession. Especially these days now, the profession is going in another direction post Wilshaw, post Michael Gove, which I liked, that era.[3]

I don't like this era so much today because it doesn't fit with me as a man, me as a person, what I believe in and the values of the Trust. I think we're losing ... I'm passionate about teaching, I'm passionate about leadership; but I think the profession is losing the plot. We're dropping our standards ...

The emphasis Wilshaw said should be on standards and curriculum. I do like that. I do like the emphasis on curriculum today. That is something that is new and I'm welcoming because kids need a balanced curriculum and, in the past, maybe it was too narrow. I'm a standards man but, maybe, it was just all standards in some schools. It needs to be developed with artistic talent. Find the talent and push it. I'm absolutely with them on that but not at the expense of standards; and standards shouldn't come at the expense of talent either. It should be both.

But what you're going towards here is a slipping of the standards, especially for white working class kids, the biggest underperforming group in the country. I feel the national agenda is tipping away from that again and we're going to be leaving these kids stood still again.

But back to your question on leadership, yeah, it starts with me as a young teacher. I was obviously open to learning but quickly recognised that I had skills that the schools I worked for, which generally were underperforming needed; because you need a bit of grit and a bit of whatever word you want to use, the government like resilience, don't they? Use that one, you need a bit of something, you need a bit of know-how and I would say the main thing you need is dedication and an interest and a concern for the job. It's not just a job. It's more than that.

There are over 600 words in Lee's opening statement (some have been excised) or, rather, his outpouring of *passion*. It is the passion of which Hattie (2012) speaks in the opening pages of his renowned *Visible Learning for Teachers*. It is the passion that I have seen, heard, witnessed in Lee's dealings with head teacher colleagues, school staff and children. It is the passion that drives him to overcome obstacles and to succeed in highly challenging circumstances. One only has to visit the sites of the six academies within The Forge Trust:

- Bowbridge estate, Newark, in which the most common council tax band is A, for The Sir Donald Bailey Academy;
- for both the Parkgate Academy and the Forest View Academy, the colliery village of New Ollerton, originally built in the mid-1920s; but times have changed with the closure of the mine 25 years ago;
- the non-ethnically diverse (98% White British) village of Rainworth for Python Hill Academy that also suffered when nearby Rufford Colliery stopped producing coal in 1993;
- Kirkby-in-Ashfield, a part of the Mansfield Urban Area for West Park Academy; and
- 5 miles south from Gainsborough, the civil parish of Marton for The Marton Academy.

Soon to be joined by a seventh school, St Augustine's in Worksop, it is noteworthy that all but two of The Forge Trust schools are currently rated 'Good' by Ofsted.[4]

Talent

But back to Lee. He speaks of talent, standards, curriculum, among others: but how does he address these? With talent – with his staff – Lee is generous. The Forge Trust fully funds Sophie Longney, the Head of Teaching and Learning as she successfully becomes one of England's first cohort of 98 teachers to achieve the prestigious award of Chartered Teacher from the Chartered College of Teaching (graduated July 2019). This is a highly demanding course and as the Chief Executive Officer (CEO) of the Chartered College of Teaching points out:

> Design and accreditation of our *CTeach* programme has been a major part of our collective endeavour to rebuild the professional status of teaching. These teachers take with them into their school confidence born out of rigorous study and a commitment to share this knowledge in the spirit of collaboration.
>
> (Lough 2019)

Words of caution however. The Chartered Teacher Scheme in Scotland attracted thousands of teachers and, whilst not flawless, was a subject of international acclaim and scrutiny (Ingvarson, 2009). Commencing with a pilot scheme in 2002, and with strong support from the Scottish Government and the 'great and good' of Scottish education; it was launched at Holyrood, the home of the *Scots Pairlament*: a decade later it was gone (Denholm, 2012).

On a dreich, winter's morning, I accompanied two other members of the Committee of the Association of Chartered Teachers Scotland, David Noble and Dorothy Coe, as we stepped warily into the imposing art deco government building that is St Andrew's House, on the southern flank of Calton Hill, Edinburgh. Our wariness stemmed from an impending unease about the future; and that was confirmed when Mike Russell, then Education Secretary, informed us that the Chartered Teacher Scheme was to be disbanded. This was despite more than two-thirds of the evidence supporting maintenance or reform of the Scheme – as opposed to less than one-third proposing disbandment. This was no evidence-based decision. Ironically, a few years later, the same Scottish Government is considering the introduction of a new 'Lead Teacher' scheme (McCall, 2019).

Thankfully, the new Chartered Teacher programme is not within the purview of UK government and remains within the hands of the teaching profession. And it is a tough programme as it requires:

> deep subject knowledge, understanding of pedagogy, assessment, and excellent classroom practice, as well as critical evaluation, engagement with research evidence ... Assessments include rigorous written and oral assignments ... professional development plan, participation in debate activities, a research-based school improvement project, and submission of a portfolio of videos of practice, work samples.
>
> (https://chartered.college/chartered-teacher)

Lee is rightly proud of his new Chartered Teacher and describes her and similar staff thus:

> I would shine their shoes for them because I think they do a marvellous job. Sophie Longney, at our place, Head of Teaching and Learning, what a practitioner, Chartered Teacher, just finished her MA. Year 6 leader, lives and breathes it, inspirational.

Lee and his senior leadership colleagues take the view that teacher professional development is to be viewed as a long-term investment and so worthy of funding. Whilst waiting for a professional conversation with Sophie, I chatted with Lee – and he was interrupted, briefly, to sign a cheque for over £3,000 to pay the university fees for a staff colleague – a *talent* – undertaking MA studies. Talent is to be nurtured and supported and this comes at a price – but the price is worth paying.

Standards

Labor Omnia Vincit – 'work conquers everything' is the motto of The Forge Trust and this derives from the context of the schools serving areas that have very high levels of unemployment and poverty. The Trust's approach is to educate the child in order to break the cycle of low aspirations leading to low attainment. Their intention is to build character and make the children competitively driven such that they want the children to be winners; but also to know how to be good losers. This was partly affirmed by the Ofsted (2018) inspection of the lead school, The Sir Donald Bailey Academy, with the inspector noting 'an emphasis [placed] on the pupils being confident and self-assured'. As CEO of The Forge Trust, Lee and his senior colleagues believe that their values clearly express these goals.

The long-term objective is to produce children who can contribute positively to society and not to have low aspirations which prevent this from happening, e.g. they have a 'dreams' board where all the children have their dreams displayed and these are shared in assemblies. The Trust heavily subsidises day and residential trips in order that no child misses out due to financial difficulties. More controversially, the pupil premium grant is directly spent on teaching staff in order to reduce class sizes and allow personalised learning; and the teaching assistant workforce has been much reduced in order to fund teaching staff. The provision of quality first teaching is seen as key to achieving the school's aims of driving up standards. As a Multi-Academy Trust, the ultimate aim is that children will benefit from an education in schools which are at least 'Good' by Ofsted criteria. The senior leadership believes that they are becoming expert in poverty; and they are very confident with regard to the effectiveness of their methods.

Whilst Lee acknowledges that their approach may be viewed as unorthodox, he points out that The Sir Donald Bailey Academy was achieving 50% Level 4+ at the end of Key Stage 2 but is now over 90%. Similarly, Ofsted (2018) records that 'the progress pupils made was above average in reading, and in both writing and mathematics it was in the top 10% of all schools nationally'. The Trust's data suggests that the attainment of these high standards will continue. This evidences their unrelenting drive to ensure quality first teaching and learning (Luby with Farrar, 2016).

Curriculum

This new focus on curriculum excites Lee and he adopts a 'hands-on' approach. Following a consultation with staff and school leaders at The Sir Donald Bailey Academy, he produced a report *The speaking & listening functional skills curriculum*. This 24-page document identifies four strands to be addressed, in particular:

- opportunities for children to show an awareness of their audience;
- opportunities for children to speak and discuss;
- opportunities for children to listen; and
- opportunities for children to practise non-verbal communication.

Each of these strands is supported by 10–14 exemplars that school staff had discussed beforehand and identifies activities and actions that require to be undertaken. Outlined in Figures 1.1–1.4 (adapted from Luby with Farrar, 2016: 21–22) those activities and actions that are *italicised* are more evident.

Role play opportunities in class is one of the exemplars for which there was very little evidence but one teacher 'bucked the trend' and spoke convincingly of how 'high ability' pupils took on different roles within group work e.g. as illustrator, leader, questioner or summariser.

A particularly good example is that of *Tinga Tinga Tales* which are African fables from You Tube (approx. 5–10 minutes long). Children's ability to listen is 'tested' by teacher questioning afterwards and by them acting out the stories. There was also notable praise for *Let's Interact*

- *To correct children and have a consistent approach by all staff.*
- *Class assemblies where children formally present information to the school.*
- *Answering registers properly – 'Good morning Miss…/Dinners please Miss…'*
- *Expectations of the children: how we speak and discipline them.*
- *House assemblies, where older children plan & deliver an assembly linked to themes of week.*
- Video blog on school website, making use of green screen technology.
- Children to meet and greet visitors and conduct school tours to potential parents.
- Children take on roles in class projects such as 'project lead'.
- Build in opportunities to speak to different audiences, making use of the community café.

Figure 1.1 Opportunities for children to show an awareness of their audience

- *Superstar Assemblies where children discuss and talk about their dreams.*
- *Circle time and 'show 'n tell' sessions.*
- *Hot seating as a teaching strategy in English.*
- *Class debates using house system, and use of talk partners in lessons.*
- Taking messages on behalf of the class teacher to other classes or departments.
- Children bring in newspapers – 'what's been happening in the week?'
- Talking Tables (early years foundation stage).

Figure1.2 Opportunities for children to speak and discuss

- *Following instructions for 'what makes a good listener'. 'Eyes looking and ears listening.'*
- *Listening to audio stories.*
- *Watching videos in lessons.*
- *Working in pairs and responding to a partner.*
- *Taking messages on behalf of staff and following instructions.*
- Note taking and actively listening for key information.
- Having a 'look out' focus and selecting three things to spot.
- Visitors coming into school to speak.
- 'Every Lesson Counts' – demonstrating excellent behaviour for learning.

Figure1.3 Opportunities for children to listen

- *Using drama and freeze frames in lessons.*
- *Children to create social stories and act them out. Pay particular attention to body language and facial expressions.*
- *Using signs and symbols in the classroom.*
- Training children for a range of contexts, e.g. when showing visitors round school children should be taught to use a firm handshake (also when leaving lessons shake teacher's hand and make eye contact).
- Using Makaton (a language programme that uses symbols, signs and speech to enable people to communicate) where applicable.
- Showing appropriate emotions and being taught these. For example, what does it look like to be angry?
- Modelling scenarios. For example, 'Your dog has died. Is it appropriate to smile?'

Figure1.4 Opportunities for children to practise non-verbal communication

Training that had been implemented several years ago and repeated by a Speech & Language therapist.

In some sense these activities and actions may appear unremarkable – with widespread use across the country – but applied consistently it moves the Ofsted inspector to comment that:

> You and your team have worked hard to improve the speaking skills of pupils across the school. In each classroom that I visited, I was greeted by two class ambassadors. These pupils shook my hand, told me their names and what they were learning in their lesson. They were consistently courteous and polite, and were obviously proud of their roles.
>
> (Ofsted 2018)

This has been a *collaborative approach* to the curriculum from Lee and his staff; each and all have opportunities to contribute - albeit there is a clear steer from senior leadership. A different, *competitive approach* is adopted, though, when it comes to the quality of teachers.

Controversy and teacher quality

A well-used adage is that 'the quality of an education system cannot exceed the quality of its teachers' which is usually attributed to the McKinsey Report, *How the world's best-performing education systems come out on top* (Barber and Mourshed, 2007). The Forge Trust takes this mantra to heart. Lee and his senior leadership team seek out the best teachers that they can find and, from their perspective, it is a small pool. In Lee's estimation only about 20% of teachers are capable of teaching well in The Forge Trust schools and he puts it bluntly:

LEE: You're probably going to disagree with me here but I do see a lot of teachers, not in my own Trust, but I do when we're … when we've taken over a school that's been underperforming I see a lot of the opposite. It's just a number for them, it's just a job, they're pulling a wage, pinching money; and I'm brave enough to say that because I love the job. I love the teaching profession and the 20% of teachers that I see that I admire and that's not a lot is it percentage but I would … shak[e] my head thinking where's it all … how's this happened? How has this been allowed to happen? Because in the world of business they'd have been sacked and that's the side of the teaching profession under the County Council regime, they get away with being weak teachers forever and a day …

   The profession … I'm going to be brave and say this because it's what I think, the profession isn't good enough, nowhere near. Twenty per cent of us live and breathe it and I'd like to think I'm one of the 20% and I'd like to think I can find that 20% out there to put in front of my kids in the schools, that's my ambition. That's what drives me on but I say to Jamie and the other key leaders around me, I'm not impressed with the profession at all. It's not a profession. It should be a profession. It should be, it's a great job, it's a great profession but it's not. I don't feel it is.

Perhaps Lee does have a jaundiced view of the teaching profession. This is understandable given that he has absorbed into The Forge Trust some schools that were deemed to be struggling. Nonetheless, I was prompted to concede that he does have a point:

AL: Uh huh. I think, … Also to back up what you say about the teachers, well I'm afraid … the Scottish Chartered Teacher Scheme people get a £7,000 pay rise. I was sitting at a conference talking to a teacher from Central Scotland and she was telling me that there were 13 Chartered Teachers in her school. I was amazed. I thought, 'Well, that's fabulous; what a great school that must be.' But then she said, 'Ah! but only two of us stick our head above the parapet and take on extra work, which is what you expect of a Chartered Teacher. The other 11 take the money and do nothing for it.'

LEE: Yeah and there is the problem isn't it?

AL: Well, that was a real blow to me being a Chartered Teacher myself ... I was just so disappointed and eventually the Chartered Teacher Scheme in Scotland was disbanded.

For Lee, and others, the truth of the matter is that some, perhaps many teachers are not 'up to the job' when it comes to teaching in challenging schools sited in areas of social deprivation. A clear problem for The Forge Trust is that from their viewpoint they are drawing upon a limited supply of teachers – with approximately only 20% sufficiently 'inspirational'. This means that they have to develop their own:

AL: How do you grow these good leaders in your own Trust then?
LEE: Well, you get back to philosophy and having a view on things aren't you? And I'm in a way of doing things; and when you're getting the NQTs [newly qualified teachers] in, you know impart that knowledge on them; and they either like or they take it in and they're sponges, or they start and think it's not for me and they leave. But when they stay, generally speaking, they don't ... they stay and the Sophie Longneys of this world ... she's the best example I can think of; but there are others, Amy Wilson at Parkgate, Emily Bonner at Python Hill: we've grown these leaders, they speak the same language as I do. 100% –
AL: So you're prepared to live with quite a high attrition rate then in order to find –
LEE: Oh yeah.
AL: Diamonds –
LEE: That's right, and that's what I hang on to Tony, to be honest; and I've got plenty of good leaders in my own Trust ...

In one sense you know the best leaders in our Trust are hard taskmasters, they have to be. But in the other sense, show me other Trusts that pay for Masters degrees, show me the Trust where your class size average is 17 so your workload is brilliant ... They've got class sizes to die for in our Trust ...

I've got plenty of staff following me, who agree with the philosophy. Laura Davis, you know Laura Davis very well, handed her notice in this week. I got a lovely letter and it's the best ... compliment I've ever had, it's the best reference I could ever have because in the letter she states inspirational leadership. I was really sorry to be going but I'm relocating, thanks for all the opportunities I've had, I've loved every minute of it, blah-blah-blah and I said to Jamie I'm putting that in a frame because I've had her from day one. So although we may sound very rigid in what I'm saying to you, these things are hard hitting at times. There's an example of somebody who has had a ball but agrees with it as well. So ...

Investment for tough love

The senior leaders at The Forge Trust, like all school leaders, only want what is best for their children. For them, though, this means that there is a limited pool of talent available and that they need to develop and invest in school teachers and leaders who *speak the same language*. It is a language of 'tough love'. They do not 'suffer fools gladly' but this is because of *compassion*. In a prior conversation, Lee was talking about visiting the first school to join their Trust. On this first visit he looked at the children in the classrooms and it was a loving look – 'these children are just like ours' he thought. And this thought drove him to establish a Multi-Academy Trust.

The Forge Trust invests significantly in their staff. Studying for a Master's degree and becoming a Chartered Teacher have significant costs but the senior leaders view this as a worthwhile investment in like-minded staff.

Like-mindedness

It is clear that the leaders of The Forge Trust identify and employ staff who identify with their values – especially the Trust motto of *Labor Omnia Vincit* – as Lee elucidates below:

LEE: And I want our kids to have a work ethic, I want them to not have an entitlement culture because I've not got it. You can say what you want about me as a man but I don't think I'm entitled to anything. I'm a grafter and I put a shift in. I'm not afraid to get my hands dirty and I will go into battle if need be. I would hate ... the biggest insult you could ever give me is workshy. He loves the Union him you know? These things just get on under my skin so I'm very opinionated about them today. But I think that's from the background, from being in Worksop. A lot of ... nine out of ten people in Worksop would tell you the opposite, we love Labour, my grandad was a miner, the other one was a miner and I think the same they got ill-treated. Arthur Scargill backed us up, and all the rest of it; and I don't see it that way. I turn it on its head. Totally on its head and that is the origins really of making you, right, what are your values? My value is a work ethic not work shyness. My values are justice, yeah I want justice but you know what I mean? That was the starting point for me as a young lad ...

AL: So how do you lead people whose opinions are at variance with yours? Don't have your background, don't have your attitude, they want to help the kids, to do the best they can.

LEE: If you're the leader, it's as Alex Ferguson said, I'm not changing, you've got to change, I'm a leader. I'm not going to change. I'll be fair with you, if you don't like it go and work somewhere else. Fergie didn't do bad did he? ... and he had a similar attitude.

AL: Some people might say that's quite a brutal attitude to ... why don't you take a more nurturing, developmental approach to your staff?

LEE: You can't ... if somebody is so opposed to you, you can't spend time trying to talk them round, you can try in the first instance; but how long are you going to spend on it, wasting your time, you've got kids to teach? You've got things to sort. Don't bother.

AL: So really the staff have to sign up to your values?

LEE: 100%. Yeah.

Advantages of this like-mindedness among the staff is that collaboration is much easier to achieve and the staff are united and working with a common purpose. Disadvantages include the limited pool of talent from which to draw upon and the very high levels of investment undertaken. Other disadvantages might be a lack of challenge from within, as everyone is so like-minded; and a lack of awareness as to what is taking place elsewhere. However, like-mindedness does not mean a close-minded approach to education and schooling; and Lee confidently handles both of these topics.

Challenge

AL: So the people in your Trust, then, for the most part are like-minded?

LEE: Yes, 100%. But they do challenge ... they will say 'Lee have you considered XYZ? We're going to hit a brick wall here.' Jamie being my number 2 is the main one who does that. But the other Principals, I've got a very good participative leadership style, so I'll go into leadership at Principal level and say what do you think to this? We'd be open about it, it's not a dictatorship. I'm leading as a Principal, alongside them as a Principal but I'm also dual role CEO so ...

AL: So, if you introduce a new policy do you put it out for consultation?

LEE: Yes. Every time.

AL: What kind of feedback do you get?

LEE: Mixed. Honest, very honest feedback, the leaders we've got are very honest they'll tell you if ... a recent example is ... I've got a view on teaching ... So, I said I want it [independent writing] weekly because the kids need to do it weekly. Forget teachers here, the kids need weekly. Put it out to my leaders and I got some opposition, 'No, bi-weekly. We want it bi-weekly.' At the end of the day what we decided was, I went with them. I said, okay, I'll go bi-weekly but don't you dare let the standards slip. I'm watching. If that standard slips it's going weekly. And do you know what, it hasn't slipped, the standard is pretty good.

AL: Bi-weekly, you mean fortnightly?

LEE: Fortnightly, yeah. But if I wanted my own way and stamped my feet I would have had it weekly. But I had enough leaders around me saying ... leaders I respected more importantly, no I think bi-weekly, we can do this bi-weekly and I went with them. Touch wood ... so far so good. Not a problem, yeah. That's just a simple example of how we operate. I have got a view and on that occasion I didn't stamp it through because too many of the leaders were telling me, 'no, we think bi-weekly'.

Lee's 'participative leadership style' is born out of a crucible of deep thinking and frustrating experience. The frustration was leading a County Council school out of special measures to a 'Good' Ofsted rating only to then 'fall out with the governing body'. This led to a head teacher post at Bowbridge primary school, Newark, which according to Lee 'was the worst performing school in Nottinghamshire in 2011, 2010; the DfE [Department for Education] had it on its radar':

AL: You go to Bowbridge, it's obviously in a poor way, how did you turn it around?

LEE: Teaching; lead by example. I could teach, model teaching, standards, expectations, you know? These job shares were going out the door at 4 minutes past 12. Pull them up; you're not doing that anymore. Everybody else who's not performing, get them on the Improvement Plan, show them how to teach, show them you can't just write people off. Show them, give them a chance, a lot of them left. Bring in new blood. Get a culture.

AL: That must have been difficult?

LEE: Very! I was rocking in the chair the first two years at night, no word of a lie, that's the effect the job has on you at times.

AL: What do you mean rocking in the chair, you were just so tired?

LEE: Not so much, I've got a chair in the room; my wife said she would often catch me just sitting staring, thinking, obviously I was thinking but it was a tough place. You had to ... any cost.

AL: Did you have any help? Was there anybody you could turn to for advice?

LEE: Not really, no, I was on my own if I'm honest. Yeah. It's a tough place. It makes you hard, you put yourself through the mill or I did. Now, I don't think that would ever happen in our Trust set up now ... but in my Trust where I'm the CEO I'm right beside ... You go down, they go down; you die, I die. That's a far better mentality than working for the County Council ... I think we've got a far better set up, outlook, camaraderie, teamwork.

This is the *tough* part of 'tough love'. For staff who were encouraged to leave and develop their career elsewhere; however, thankfully, 'they've been fine ever since'. Tough, also, for Lee; although many may regard it to be self-inflicted as he chose to go down this road. But, for Lee and his colleagues, it is all about the children. And when you visit The Forge Trust schools it is hard not to be impressed. And when Lee reels off statistics concerning the performance of The Forge Trust schools ...

AL: But the first school you took on, was that Parkgate, it changed its name to Parkgate?

LEE: Yeah fantastic! That's the biggest ... that's probably the thing I'm ... as well as being proud of Donald Bailey and everything we achieve there, in terms of the map, that's my proudest achievement. I mean that was underperforming for 20 years and it had a deficit budget, massive deficit budget. They've got 200 grand in reserves, they've got class sizes of 17 throughout the board, they've got two or three doing MAs ...

    Superb! A brilliant young head teacher in Mark Nunn, that I'm proud to have helped develop; he's got his own mind but I've mentored him ... although he's got his own mind, agrees on the main things to do with the Trust, how we run schools, agrees on the philosophy of managing the staff, agrees on the teaching philosophy.

    When we took it over they had 190 pupils on roll, today they've got 330 and growing. The place is really rocking. The results at Parkgate were well below the national average, progress measures were poor, today they're above the national average, massive upward trend every year and outcomes are better, so outcomes are an evidence base and I would guess the other one is the ... you go and look round the place, it was a poor building, let's say, to put it politely. We've invested some of the money we've been able to save; we've invested it back in the buildings.

    Donald Bailey again failing, bottom results wise in 2011, now ... we're the best performing school in Newark year on year, three and four year averages and we haven't been the best in attainment yet, we've been up there but this year projections are a bit like a crystal ball but our projections are based on evidence. This year we'll hit 80% combined attainment when the national average is 67, so ... We've no reason it shouldn't because we've already done mocks if you like with last papers and it was 80 odd. So there's no reason it won't come in. So results are obviously up.

The participative leadership style of The Forge Trust does address a perceived disadvantage of like-mindedness lacking *challenge* as the school Principals do embrace challenge. Indeed, the success of this Trust is evident to see and, on a regular basis, it receives offers, recommendations and requests to join – and these are regularly turned down; although, shortly, a seventh school will become a member. A second topic of disadvantage that has been identified is that of like-mindedness entailing a close-minded approach – but Lee's response is 'research'.

Research

AL: So how do you develop your staff then in terms of professional development, what would you look for, what would you provide for them?

LEE: Research.

AL: Who does the research?

LEE: Leaders mainly and teachers; and develop the young teachers and get two or three in each school, MAs for example, that's one way which you know I do. But there are other routes as well, other courses we sign up for … You don't want your … you don't want too many steady teachers.

AL: What do you mean by steady teacher?

LEE: Not interested in research because a lot of them aren't. We don't want them. They're not going to push boundaries especially in the hardest schools which you know we have … We need the best teachers. So if you've got a school full of Steady Eddie's that's not going to … you're not going to get the results. You're not going to get the impact for the kids. Somebody bringing in … policies getting changed, made better and better and better, you go stale.

Lee's enthusiasm for research derives partly from his own successful MA Education Studies with Bishop Grosseteste University, Lincoln. He encourages and develops this through staff sponsorship for MA studies and the aforementioned *CTeach* course with the Chartered College of Teaching. He wants his staff to embrace research and scholarship and Lee leads by example. And his desire is for research and scholarship to inform teaching – and, as a Trust leader, he retains an active interest in teaching:

LEE: I can still teach thankfully, touch wood, otherwise the day I lose that ability to have a view on teaching them I'm totally reliant on other people as a top leader. You don't want to be that; you want to have a view so you know what's going off. And one of the recent things was writing, independent writing, and I have a view from being a teacher that if you give kids a content to write, be simplistic about it. Give them an interesting context, they'll write, you've obviously got to teach them in English lessons by modelling their writing. Shared writing is the biggest impact for me anyway, shared writing. And the marking and feedback, if it's diagnostic and builds on previous learning, it's still important despite what they're saying about workload. You can't get rid of that for me, if you want top writers, but the issue was 'do we write once a week or twice a week?' Because from a workload point of view diagnostic marking takes time and what if you've got 20 of these books to mark? Well, I as a teacher didn't even blink; I did it with 17-20 kids and more.

Ultimately, it is about pedagogy and what transpires in the classroom and the structures that are in place to support good pedagogic practices and as Stoll (2015: 21) puts it: 'Pedagogy is at the core and leadership and professional development are there to ensure that pedagogy is great. But great pedagogy also challenges and inspires leadership and professional development to new heights.'

Stoll uses the term *self-improving school system* and claims that pedagogy, leadership and professional development lie at the heart of a successful system. There are many examples of good pedagogic practices across The Forge Trust and this is supported by a senior leadership that is willing to invest heavily. They do so with regard to pedagogy as evidenced by the small class sizes and for the staff with respect to MA courses, *CTeach* and the like. It can be described as a *competitive-collaborative model*. The Trust bears a *competitive* hallmark with respect to recruiting and retaining high-quality staff; and it is *collaborative* through its like-mindedness and levels of investment.

The notion that The Forge Trust perceives itself to be a *self-improving school system* can be summed up by Lee's response to my question inviting comparison between a Multi-Academy Trust and local authority schools:

LEE: When push comes to shove you're on your own. They'll all help you; they'll (local authority) give you this and that but at the end of the day if results fail whose head is on the block? Now in a Trust set up what we actually say in our Trust is listen there shouldn't be one head around the table who's sitting with their head in their hands one year; because if that happened we've all got to look at ourselves. All of us; because we share everything. So this school shouldn't be that much different to that one in theory because we share everything. We share staff across the Trust. We've got network meetings in core subjects and other subjects as well now. So from a CEO point of view if a head has got their head in their hands, so have I. Take a look in the mirror, does that happen at the local authority level?

So, let us follow Lee's advice and look at two local authorities that are trying to close the attainment gap through educational practices. This takes us back to the land of my heart: Scotland – and to the areas in which I grew up: the city of Glasgow and the shire of Renfrew.

Afterword

When undertaking the original research with the Ad Astra Primary Partnership it soon became self-evident that these schools were 'pursu[ing] issues and change initiatives that are relevant to their own setting and context' (Hammersley-Fletcher et al., 2015:5) i.e. poverty and underachievement. I soon surmised that the role of the researcher was to use a process that enabled the Ad Astra schools to quickly become better informed about their current progress; and I deemed this research process to be that of *professional conversations*. These conversations derive from the work of Stenhouse (1975:157) who was concerned 'with the development of a self-critical subjective perspective [and] not with an aspiration towards an unattainable objectivity'. To illustrate:

The Sir Donald Bailey Academy was addressing the area of 'Poverty of Language' and had identified 4 strands for developing 'Speaking and Listening' – one of which is 'Awareness of Audience'. During a professional conversation one of the teachers spoke of how she helped to prepare pupils for presenting at school assemblies through paired discussions in the classroom. It seemed to the lead researcher that the pupils' awareness of audience could be developed by the teacher adopting the 'snowballing' technique advocated by Noel Entwistle for higher education; but now widely prevalent in the literature of education (e.g. Atkins et al 2002; Jones 2007; Wahyuni 2013). The classroom teacher was open and receptive (self-critical) in her thinking (subjective perspective) and commented that she had enjoyed the conversation and would use this technique with her pupils.

(Luby with Farrar 2016:18)

As it is a two-way conversation then there is a *process* of sharing. If the researcher has information or an experience that will be of help to the teacher, then it should be shared. It is *research for transformation* and not research as knowledge. With the latter, 'the disinterested, objective researcher is in pursuit of knowledge – and this is exemplified through the writing of journal papers and academic books' (Luby, 2016a: 3). But in the immediacy of this conversation with a classroom teacher who is preparing her children for presenting at school assemblies; then the prime concern of this researcher is transformation. Why?

From an educational perspective, the relationship between research and teaching is not merely acquisition of knowledge – rather, as expressed by Pring (2000:14, emphasis added), 'education refers to that learning which in some way *transforms* how people see and value things, how they understand and make sense of experience, how they can identify and solve key problems'. Imparting and sharing information about the 'snowballing' technique was to help her recognise that I value her strategy of paired discussions; that a similar experience can assist her with this problem.

At the very least, it is an attempt to empathise with the classroom teacher. From a *modern* perspective, Dadds (2005: 31) admonishes researchers that 'we must remember that we are ... stepping into others' lives – and our actions must make sense to them ... we need to move ... into an empathetic perspective'. And so, there is a need to empathise with the classroom teacher and share her concerns. Further, from a *classic* perspective and drawing upon Aristotle, Bernstein (1983:147) states that:'The person with understanding does not know and judge as one who stands apart and unaffected; but rather, as one united by a specific bond with the other, thinks with the other and undergoes the situation with the other.' Therefore, empathy is a necessary attribute if one is to gain genuine understanding and it is helpful to achieve this 'specific bond' or 'fellowship' (Luby, 2016a) if one is or has been a practising classroom teacher. This view of research as transformation is also found outside of the discipline of education as evidenced by Brew (2001:25) who identified four modes of researchers' thinking with regard to research; the last of which is 'research is interpreted as a personal journey of discovery, possibly leading to transformation'.

Dialogue capturing the process of transformation

This transformative process involves much tacit, implicit and experiential knowledge and, as Sharples (2013), points out, 'It is important to remember that there is a huge amount of experiential knowledge that is not captured by research.' Indeed, I only have to think of three friends with lengthy careers in teaching – between them they have more than 100 years of experiential knowledge and, until now, none of it has been captured by research (Luby, 2016a). However, they can certainly talk about their processes of transformation from beginning teachers to experienced, successful teachers and senior leaders. And dialogue provides a key to unlocking and capturing this process of transformation. Drawing upon the works of such as Lieberman and Miller (2001) and Richardson (1997), Tillema and Orland-Barak (2006:594) discuss a reflective view on the nature of professional knowledge which 'regards professionals' construction of shared knowledge as an exchange of individual personal, implicit knowledge that becomes explicit (less tacit) through social exchange and dialogue thus distributed as professional knowledge'. The above illustration from The Sir Donald Bailey Academy is such an example.

The conversations were intended to be relaxed, casual and a two-way process but with the large majority of the talking coming from the conversation partner. A brief look at the transcripts indicates that the latter intention was achieved and weaknesses with respect to the first intention are the fault of the writer alone. There were no pre-prepared questions for the conversations but if partners asked beforehand about topics, then they were informed that pedagogy, professional development and leadership (Stoll, 2015) were of interest.

During the conversations, opportunities were sought for cumulative talk and exploratory talk. In order to empathise with a conversation partner it is useful to engage with cumulative talk which entails 'build[ing] positively but uncritically on what the other has said' (Mercer, 1995:104). In the above conversation with Lee Hessey, for instance, he makes a controversial statement that for some teachers, 'it's just a number for them, it's just a job, they're pulling a wage, pinching money'. I countered with the comment about the 11 Chartered Teachers in the Scottish school who were doing likewise. This was to reassure Lee and let him know that I understood his point and empathised with his disappointment regarding some teacher colleagues.

Also sought were opportunities for exploratory talk that involves 'engag[ing] critically but constructively with each other's ideas' (Mercer, 1995:104). Shortly after the above extract from the conversation with Lee, I criticise Lee's stance by claiming 'But that can't be typical … you're seeing a school that's struggling; other people turn around and say, "well, what about all the good schools out there that you don't see?"' My criticism is that Lee's view of the teaching profession may be somewhat jaundiced since as CEO of The Forge Trust he is more aware of struggling schools than he is of good or outstanding schools. Lee takes this in his stride and comments:

> teachers who've left Donald Bailey to go elsewhere for example, where it hasn't worked out for them, they've been absolutely fine elsewhere; but I wouldn't have wanted them for too long because they didn't have the ingredients that I wanted for our children at Donald Bailey. So, generally speaking, I think the acceptable level that's out there isn't high enough but it's good enough for the profession at the minute because we've got a teacher shortage.
>
> (Lee 2019)

This Afterword draws attention to the desire of Lawrence Stenhouse for the development of a practitioner's self-critical subjective perspective. Such development can take place in isolation – through scholarship for example – but I affirm the contention of Reason and Rowan

(1981: 242) that this self-critical subjective perspective can be enhanced and strengthened to become 'inter-subjectively valid knowledge which is beyond the limitations of one knower'.[5] A professional conversation is one means of achieving this.

Notes

1 Bassetlaw is the electoral constituency that had the largest swing nationally of 18% from Labour to the Conservatives at the 2019 UK General Election (source: *The Sunday Times*, 15 December 2019). This is of significance given the tenor of Lee Hessey's political comments.
2 Methodologically speaking, the professional conversations outlined within this book are *unstructured interviews* – but more is said about this in the Afterword.
3 Presumably, Lee was heartened to read in the *Times Education Supplement* that 'The Gove gang are back in business' (Dorrell, 2019).
4 Two of the schools were previously deemed 'Inadequate' and were subsequently closed prior to becoming new members of The Forge Trust.
5 As quoted in Dadds (2005: 32).

References

Atkins, M., Brown, G. A. and Brown, G. 2002. *Effective Teaching in Higher Education*. Abingdon, Oxon: Routledge.

Barber, M. and Mourshed, M. 2007. [Online] *How the world's best-performing school systems come out on top*. September 2007. Available from: www.mckinsey.com/industries/social-sector/our-insights/how-the-worlds-best-performing-school-systems-come-out-on-top [Accessed 22 July 2019]

Bernstein, R. J. 1983. *Beyond Objectivism and Relativism: Science, Hermeneutics, and Praxis*. Philadelphia: University of Pennsylvania Press.

Brew, A. 2001. *The Nature of Research: Inquiry in Academic Contexts*. London: Routledge/Falmer.

Dadds, M. 2005. Taking curiosity seriously. In K. Sheehy, M. Nind, J. Rix and K. Simmons (Eds) *Ethics and Research in Inclusive Education: Values into Practice*. Abingdon, Oxon: Routledge/Falmer.

Denholm, A. 2012. [Online] 'Superteacher' scheme to be axed. *The Herald*. 28 January 2012. Available from: www.heraldscotland.com/news/13045829.superteacher-scheme-to-be-axed/ [Accessed 20 July 2019]

Dorrell, E. 2019. [Online] The Gove gang are back in business. *Times Education Supplement*. 8 August 2019. Available from: www.tes.com/news/gove-gang-are-back-business [Accessed 12 August 2019]

Hammersley-Fletcher, L. and Lewin, C. with Davies, C., Duggan, J., Rowley, H. and Spink, E. 2015. [Online] *Evidence-based teaching: advancing capability and capacity for enquiry in schools*. Interim report: Autumn 2015. Nottingham: National College Teaching and Leadership (NCTL). Available from: www.gov.uk/government/publications/evidence-based-teaching-advancing-capability-and-capacity-for-enquiry-in-schools-interim-report [Accessed 20 July 2019]

Hattie, J. 2012. *Visible Learning for Teachers: Maximizing Impact on Learning*. Abingdon, Oxon: Routledge.

Ingvarson, L. 2009. Developing and rewarding excellent teachers: the Scottish Chartered Teacher Scheme. *Professional Development in Education* 35(3) 451-468.

Jones, R. W. 2007. Learning and teaching in small groups: characteristics, benefits, problems and approaches. *Anaesthesia and Intensive Care* 35(4) 587-592.

Lancashire, S. 2019. [Online] Book review: Imperfect Leadership. *Times Education Supplement*. 14 July 2019. Available from: www.tes.com/news/book-review-imperfect-leadership [Accessed 18 July 2019]

Lieberman, A. and Miller, L. 2001. *Teachers Caught in the Action: Professional Development That Matters*. New York: Teachers College Press.

Lough, C. 2019. [Online] First teachers to achieve chartered status. *Times Education Supplement*. 19 July 2019. Available from: www.tes.com/news/first-teachers-achieve-chartered-status [Accessed 20 July 2019]

Luby, A. 2016a. Stars and saints: professional conversations for enhancing classroom practices. *Education Today: Journal of The College of Teachers* 66(3) 2-6.

Luby, A. (Ed.) 2016b. *Poverty and Closing the Gap: Ad Astra Research Consultancy Projects*. Lincoln: Bishop Grosseteste University.

Luby, A. 2019. To the stars: Ad Astra addressing poverty. In P. Beckley (Ed.) *Supporting Vulnerable Children in Early Years: Practical Guidance and Strategies for Working with Children at Risk*. London: Jessica Kingsley.

Luby, A. and Beckley, P. 2019. A modern tale from the Sherwood Forest. *Researching Education Bulletin*. [Electronic] Issue 8, 8–11, Spring 2019. Available from: www.sera.ac.uk/wp- content/uploads/sites/13/2019/03/SERA-REB-iss-8-Spring-2019-FINAL-pdf.pdf [Accessed 22 July 2019]

Luby, A. with Farrar, E. 2016. The Sir Donald Bailey Academy: speaking & listening skills. In A. Luby (Ed.) *Poverty and Closing the Gap: Ad Astra Research Consultancy Projects*. Lincoln: Bishop Grosseteste University, 17–24.

McCall, C. 2019. [Online] Teachers in Scotland to be offered more 'flexible' career options. *The Scotsman*. 31 May 2019. Available from: www.scotsman.com/news/politics/teachers-in-scotland-to-be-offered-more-flexible-career-options-1-4938903 [Accessed 20 July 2019]

Mercer, N. 1995. *The Guided Construction of Knowledge: Talk amongst Teachers and Learners*. Cleveden, Avon: Multilingual Matters Ltd.

Munby, S. 2019. *Imperfect Leadership: A Book for Leaders Who Know They Don't Know It All*. Carmarthen: Crown House Publishing.

Ofsted. 2018. *Short inspection of The Sir Donald Bailey Academy*. March 2018. Available from: https://files.api.ofsted.gov.uk/v1/file/2762679 [Accessed 22 July 2019]

Pring, R. 2000. *Philosophy of Educational Research*. London: Continuum.

Puttick, S., Hill, Y., Beckley, P., Farrar, E., Luby, A. and Hounslow-Eyre, A. 2020. Liminal spaces around primary schools in predominantly white working-class areas in England. *Ethnography and Education* 15(2) 137–154. https://doi.org/10.1080/17457823.2018.1564062 [Accessed 22 April 2020]

Reason, P. and Rowan, J. 1981. Issues of validity in new paradigm research. In P. Reason and J. Rowan (Eds) *Human Inquiry*. Chichester: John Wiley.

Richardson, V. 1997. *Constructivist Teacher Education: Building a World of New Understandings*. London: The Falmer Press.

Sharples, J. 2013. [Online] *Evidence for the frontline*. London: Alliance for Useful Evidence. Available from: www.alliance4usefulevidence.org/assets/EVIDENCE-FOR-THE-FRONTLINE-FINAL-5-June-2013.pdf [Accessed 29 July 2019]

Stenhouse, L. 1975. *An Introduction to Curriculum Research and Development*. London: Heinemann.

Stoll, L. 2015. [Online] *Three greats for a self-improving school system – pedagogy, professional development and leadership: research report*. Nottingham: National College for Teaching & Leadership (NCTL). Available from: https://assets.publishing.service.gov.uk/government/uploads/system/uploads/attachment_data/file/406278/Three_greats_for_a_self_improving_system_pedagogy_professional_development_and_leadership_full_report.pdf [Accessed 25 July 2019]

Tillema, H. and Orland-Barak, L. 2006. Constructing knowledge in professional conversations: the role of beliefs on knowledge and knowing. *Learning and Instruction* 16(2006) 592–608.

Wahyuni, S. 2013. The use of snowballing strategy in teaching reading literary texts (short stories). *Language Circle: Journal of Language and Literature* 7(2) 53–63.

2 Caledonia rising
The Scottish Attainment Challenge

Introduction

In a famous poem Robert Burns ponders, 'O wad some Power the giftie gie us; To see oursels as ithers see us!' And how do others see us? As inhabitants of the world's most beautiful country as voted by *Rough Guides*?[1] A home to four ancient universities – St Andrew's, Glasgow, Aberdeen and Edinburgh? As creators of Europe's first national system of education – the mythologised *lad o' pairts*? In more recent times, the arrival in 1965 of the General Teaching Council Scotland as the first professional registration body for teachers in the UK and, indeed, one of the first teaching councils in the world. These are some of the factors contributing to 'Scotland ha[ving] an historic high regard for education' (OECD, 2015).

But how do we *'see oursels'*? Sentimentally, we are proud of our history and our native land. Educationally, we are proud of our comprehensive system introduced in 1968. For the most part, local children attend local schools with only 7% of the school population attending fee-paying independent schools. But all is not well. The doyen of Scottish education policy, Professor Lindsay Paterson at the University of Edinburgh, writes a controversially titled blog – *Scotland's Curriculum for Excellence: the betrayal of a whole generation?* According to Paterson (2018) Scotland's system of education:

> is now mediocre. That decline is most evident in ... the Programme for International Student Assessment ... Scotland used to be well ahead of the OECD average. It has now sunk to average, not only because other places have advanced rapidly but also because there has been *an absolute Scottish decline* [emphasis added].

And, sadly, there is worse to come: our native land is not so beautiful after all. A national tabloid newspaper, the *Daily Record*, reports a major academic study into 120,000 neighbourhoods in the UK which finds that 59 of the worst-hit 100 housing estates for poverty and inequality are in Scotland (Silvester, 2018). This study by Professor Lloyd from the University of Liverpool analysed council wards across Britain, narrowing areas down to 'cells' of small neighbourhoods measuring one square kilometre. Incredibly, of the 23 worst areas in the UK, 20 were in Glasgow and one each in Greenock, Paisley and Rutherglen.

Let Glasgow flourish

In response to these shocking statistics, Glasgow City Council leader Susan Aitken adapted the city's motto and painted a positive future for Glasgow citizens: 'Our vision is very much to have a world class city with a thriving, inclusive, economy where everyone can flourish and benefit from the city's success' (Silvester, 2018). At first glance, this seems like a glib political response – but her preceding remark indicates an understanding of the problem and how it can be addressed: 'Glasgow's deep-seated and complex deprivation issues require a long-term, cohesive, multi-stranded approach to eradicating poverty in the city by helping to create a more sustainable and inclusive economy for all of our citizens' (Silvester, 2018). And education is but one strand – albeit a highly important strand – in the City of Glasgow's multifaceted response. How successful has this response been? Let the figures speak for themselves – see Table 2.1.

In England the 'gold standard' is the A-level and for Scotland it is the Higher Grade. In both measures listed in Table 2.1 with respect to Higher Grades, pupil performance has more than doubled in the 11 years from 2007 until 2018. These findings alone justify the claim of the City of Glasgow's convener for education, Chris Cunningham, that: 'The improvements in the learning and teaching in our schools are nothing short of remarkable and the report today is proof of these achievements' (Hepburn, 2019). The March 2019 report to which he refers is from Education Scotland[2] and it is titled *Inspection of local authorities. How well is Glasgow City Council improving learning, raising attainment and closing the poverty-related attainment gap?* (Education Scotland, 2019b). This report lays bare some sobering facts about education in Scotland's largest city. More than a quarter of all children in Scotland who live in Scottish Index of Multiple Deprivation (SIMD) levels 1 and 2, the highest levels of deprivation, attend a Glasgow school. Significantly, this results in many Glasgow schools having most or almost all of their children living in the most deprived communities in Scotland.

The city of Glasgow has not been left alone to cope with these levels of deprivation and their impact upon educational provision. In 2015 the Scottish Government introduced the Scottish Attainment Challenge which is a programme to raise attainment, improve learning and reduce the impact of poverty on educational outcomes for learners. Within this national programme, Glasgow City Council is one of the nine Challenge Authorities. The Attainment

Table 2.1 Key figures for education in Glasgow

	2007	2013	2018
Students achieving one or more Higher Grade by the end of S5 (Y12)	28.0%		56.2%
Students achieving five or more Higher Grades by the end of S5 (Y12)	5.0%		13.5%
School leavers with one or more Higher Grade		50.5%	64.4%
School leavers with five or more Higher Grades		20.7%	28.2%
School leavers going onto higher education	21.7%		38.9%

Source: Hepburn (2019)

Scotland Fund has a total budget of £750 million over a six-year period from 2015 and 'as a Challenge Authority, Glasgow City Council is allocated a very significant proportion of this funding' (Education Scotland, 2019b:1).

In December 2018, HM Inspectors and other professionals evaluated the City Council's education service's strategies to close the attainment gap for those living in areas of high deprivation. This inspection included quality indicators for the evaluation of improvements in performance, leadership and management, and self-evaluation. During the inspection the focus was on two key areas, namely:

1. the effectiveness of data usage 'to target, select and evaluate the impact of initiatives'; and
2. the effectiveness of 'leadership, governance and management of resources to improve learning, raise attainment and mitigate impact of poverty on learner outcomes' (Education Scotland, 2019b:1).

Effective use of data

As its own *Glasgow: a learning city, annual service plan and improvement report 2018-2019*[3] makes clear, Glasgow City Council and its schools have a sophisticated approach with respect to data usage. They use a variety of tools such as:

Insight – a national benchmarking and reporting tool that enables comparison of Glasgow pupils' performance with a virtual comparator i.e. pupils from schools in other local authorities who have similar characteristics.

Broad General Education (BGE) Improvement Tool – implemented in 2018 this has a similar function as *Insight* but with respect to the broad general education of S1–S3 (Y8–10) pupils. It enables analysis of the achievement of *Curriculum for Excellence* (CfE) data through use of a number of pupil characteristics considered to have an influence on attainment.

FOCUS – launched in 2017, this interactive, web-based tool, owned and developed by Glasgow City Council also helps schools to examine pupil achievement of CfE. It operates a number of lenses including EAL (English as an additional language), deprivation (Social Index of Multiple Deprivation), ethnicity and others. Comparator schools are provided for benchmarking purposes (ten for primary schools and five for secondary schools). Feedback suggests that it is particularly useful for identifying gaps in pupil attainment and targeting the use of pupil equity funding.[4]

The West Partnership – a collaborative arrangement between eight local authorities i.e.:
East Dunbartonshire Council;
East Renfrewshire Council;
Glasgow City Council;
Inverclyde Council;
North Lanarkshire Council;
Renfrewshire Council;
South Lanarkshire Council; and
West Dunbartonshire Council.

This partnership is involved with developing key education performance measures and targets across the West of Scotland that can be used to target support and improve the quality of education provision. That this collaborative arrangement appears to be working is partly evidenced by the two recent, successful HMI inspections undertaken with West Dunbartonshire Council and Renfrewshire Council (rated 'very good' and 'excellent' respectively). It is to be hoped, though, that it does not replicate the English experience 'with the ensuing obsession with data that has helped drive many out of the profession' (George, 2019).

Raising attainment and mitigating impact of poverty on learners

In March 2019, HM Inspectors confidently declared that 'Glasgow City Council is making excellent progress in improving learning, raising attainment and mitigating the impact of poverty on learners' (Education Scotland, 2019b: 17) A prime reason for this assertion lies in the preparedness of the city council. With responsibility for 30 secondary schools, 138 primary schools and 275 other centres of learning, Glasgow City Council was, indeed, well prepared for this inspection as evidenced by the production of *Glasgow's Improvement Challenge*.[5] In this document, the city council pledges to:

- raise attainment in literacy and numeracy;
- improve children's health and wellbeing;
- support families to be enabled to support their child's learning and development;
- enhance the leadership of staff at all levels; and
- raise attainment in secondary schools with a continued focus on improving learning and teaching.

According to HM Inspectors, Glasgow City Council's 'aspirational agenda is focused on addressing the barriers created by child poverty ... (as) it is firmly founded in *strong evidence-based practice*, promoting high-quality learning and teaching in educational provision across the city' (Education Scotland, 2019b: 3, emphasis added). What is the basis of this strong evidence-based practice? A variety of programmes such as 'Making Thinking Visible', 'Pedagogy and Equity', 'Co-operative Learning' and the development of Teaching Learning Communities (TLCs). Let us examine a few in some detail. At a foundational level is literacy and numeracy and for Glasgow City Council this is represented by 'Literacy for All' and 'Glasgow Counts' (see Table 2.2 and Figure 2.1).

Informed by experience, Glasgow City Council claims that Literacy for All (LfA) offers Career-Long Professional Learning (CLPL)[6] that helps teachers to provide high-quality, *evidence-based approaches* to improving reading, writing and listening & talking. For Glasgow, closing the attainment gap requires creative and innovative approaches such as engagement through film literacy in order to take account of children's experiences and interests both at school and at home.

A key feature again, shared with LfA, is the use of high-quality CLPL to enable practitioners to build capacity in their establishments. There seems to be an almost relentless focus on evidence-based practices for which there are sufficient evidences of classroom worthiness that they are 'rolled out' to other classroom practitioners. Evidence for the worthiness of

Table 2.2 Glasgow's Improvement Challenge: Literacy

LITERACY for ALL (LfA)		
Reading	*Reading into Writing*	*Listening & Talking*
Phonological awareness and Reading Readiness	Early writing; Writing Strategies	Word Aware
Reading strategies	Spelling; Non-fiction texts	Addressing the vocabulary gap
Close reading; Early reading	Approaches to assessment	Group talk; Discursive talk and debating
Digital literacy	Fiction texts; Enjoyment and choice	Developing talk through play and active learning
Critical literacy	Meeting learners' needs	Meeting learners' needs
Film literacy	Creating multimodal texts	Short talks and responding to texts
Enjoyment and choice		
Scotland reads		

Source: www.glasgow.gov.uk/CHttpHandler.ashx?id=44070&p=0

GLASGOW COUNTS

> MATHS MINDSET + CPA (Concrete, Pictorial, Abstract) + PROBLEM SOLVING + MATHS TALK + VISIBLE THINKING + MEETING LEARNERS' NEEDS

GLASGOW COUNTS aims to fill young minds with a sense of agency and endow them with the motivation, courage and belief in their power to influence their own futures. We want our young people to engage with mathematics and build their comprehension of the subject across the curriculum. In addition, we aim to build better mathematical understanding in and beyond our classrooms.

The *Glasgow Counts* key messages are:

- to use the CPA approach to develop mathematical understanding;
- to develop problem solving, reasoning and fluency;
- to create mathematical mind-sets;
- to develop mastery learning;
- to engage in Maths Talk;
- to meet the needs of all learners.

Key messages are communicated through high-quality Career-Long Professional Learning (CLPL) which enables practitioners to build capacity in their establishments. In making what is sometimes seen as complex accessible, we are steadily debunking the popular myth that there is such a thing as being 'no good at Maths'.

Recently, we augmented our existing programme with a comprehensive package which aids understanding and implementation of Number Talks. In collaboration with the Leaders of Early Learning and our secondary school colleagues we now have 3 interleaving programmes: Glasgow Counts in our playrooms, primaries and secondaries, providing full coverage of the 3–18 curriculum. We have also increased partnership working.

Figure 2.1 Glasgow's Improvement Challenge: Numeracy
Source: www.glasgow.gov.uk/CHttpHandler.ashx?id=44069&p=0

such evidence-based practices as LfA and Glasgow Counts is affirmed by the comment of Education Scotland's strategic director of scrutiny, Janie McManus, that 'What stood out in this report were the approaches to targeting, selecting and evaluating the impact of initiatives' (Hepburn, 2019). Taking a long-term view of educational outcomes, as depicted in Table 2.1, the evidence is impressive that Glasgow is making real progress in a city infamous for its levels of material deprivation.

But Glasgow is not alone in encountering deprivation and, sometimes, it is found in seemingly, unlikely places.

Trialling in the Vale

The approach to scrutiny adopted by Education Scotland was first trialled with West Dunbartonshire Council in December 2017. This local authority is responsible for 5 secondary schools, 33 primary schools, and 33 other centres and learning partnerships for children; and encompassed within this region is the *Vale of Leven*. The name itself conjures up a bucolic image of rolling fields and hills – but nothing could be further from the truth: in two contrasting ways.

First, the Vale of Leven is a hotch-potch of council housing schemes built in different eras. At its heart is to be found the exotically named village of Alexandria – but there is little that is exotic in the unkemptness other than, perhaps, the shell of the 'Torpedo Factory' that is now a front for a variety of business enterprises. The Mill of Haldane, Jamestown, Bonhill, Renton are the places with which the local people identify as each has its own identity. My views of each are prejudiced. The former is where I lived in digs with the down-to-earth Kinsella family. Well-fed, lovingly looked-after by Eddie and Isa; a happy year. My first post as a young policeman in the glorious summer of 1976. Jamestown – 'toughened up' by my shift sergeant (literally, a 'breaking-in' of boots) as I plodded this beat hour-upon-hour. Bonhill, high up the hillside and overlooking the town; a housing scheme of new homes provided by the Scottish Special Housing Association (SSHA) – and my aunt Cathy and uncle Phil were proud to live in a SSHA home and rear their loving family. Renton – historic, famous even within the world of football[7] – but with a threatening undertone.

Second, the stunning beauty. The Vale of Leven incorporates Balloch, now Gateway to the Loch Lomond and Trossachs national park. Several hours, tail-ending a long night-shift were spent gazing upon the beauty of 'yon bonnie banks and yon bonnie braes' from within the confines of a panda car. Beauty. How can data, figures, learning outcomes do justice to the richness of human experience? Each and every life is rich – in different ways – some enlightening, some tragic – but all worthy of honour. And this is what teachers do – pay honour to children, not only as they are but also to whom they might become. Is this not difficult, dispiriting? Yes, can be, often. But teaching is also uplifting, rewarding, fulfilling – not all of the time – but enough of the time to make it worthy of the commitment.

But that was more than 40 years ago – a generation apart – surely, it has changed? Yes, but not by that much. The infrastructure is broadly the same. The features of the Vale of Leven are broadly recognisable. The overgrowth where I cornered a cowardly assailant; surprisingly, still there. The small, private housing estate, locus of my first arrest – an upset brother-in-law wielding an axe to an unyielding front door; unsurprisingly, still there. Eddie and Isa, Cathy and Phil, sadly, no longer with us in this realm. But the latters' requiem masses confirm that the people, broadly speaking are still the same. Less religious, without doubt, but still of sound stock and warm heart. However ...

Back to the numbers ...

The Scottish Index of Multiple Deprivation tells us:

> that just under half of all pupils in West Dunbartonshire Council schools live in the areas of highest deprivation categorised as SIMD 1 and 2. This is well above the national average. The percentage living in SIMD areas 3 and 4 is also above the national average.
>
> (Education Scotland 2018)

With respect to primary schooling, the West Dunbartonshire Council drew upon £3.3 million from the Attainment Scotland Fund between late 2015 and mid-2018 in order to fund Scottish Attainment Challenge initiatives. Funding for secondary schools began in the 2016-2017 financial year and between 2016 and 2018 West Dunbartonshire Council drew upon just over £1.1 million from the Attainment Scotland Fund. Additionally, the Pupil Equity Fund was introduced in 2017 and this forms part of the £750 million Attainment Scotland Fund that will be available until academic session 2020-2021. In 2017-2018, a total of £3.4 million has been provided to head teachers in West Dunbartonshire although only £2 million was spent (with the remainder being carried over). That it was spent wisely is affirmed by Education Scotland which poses the question 'How effective is the education service's use of data to target, select and evaluate the impact of initiatives?' In response, it finds that:

> The education service makes very good use of data to target improvement initiatives funded through the Scottish Attainment Challenge and Pupil Equity Funding. Overall, strong self-evaluation at all levels has resulted in evidence-based targeted interventions to secure improvement in learning, raise attainment and close the poverty-related attainment gap ...
>
> The local authority structure of local learning communities facilitates strong collaborative planning for professional learning ... [and] there is a supportive environment for discussion of data and improvement strategies. This is leading to an increasingly strong culture of distributed leadership and practitioner responsibility to improve outcomes in literacy, numeracy and ... in addition, high quality professional learning has significantly increased staff skills including ... data analysis and effective pedagogy. Staff have deepened their understanding of the poverty related attainment gap. The growing use of collaborative action research is supporting staff to base developments on research, local and national policy and what is considered to be good practice.
>
> (Education Scotland 2018: 6)

There is much that is commendable and praiseworthy within these findings by Education Scotland: evidence-based targeted interventions, structure of local learning communities, strong culture of distributed leadership, growing use of collaborative action research, etc. However, the actual evidence of improvement within the report is 'thin on the ground' being restricted to comments like 'Early qualitative data is promising regarding improved outcomes for children ... Although it will be some time before robust quantitative data can be used to measure the impact of these initiatives' (Education Scotland, 2018: 7). Nonetheless, if one drills down into the background reports such as by the West Dunbartonshire Psychological Service (WDPS) (2017) then one finds some convincing, supportive data.

The WDPS report furnishes evidence of four initiatives i.e.

1. Scottish Attainment Challenge Primary Project: Transitions 1– Creating a family learning hub pre-school to primary to help narrow the poverty-related attainment gap;
2. Scottish Attainment Challenge Secondary Project: Establishing multi-agency hubs in Clydebank High School and Our Lady & St Patrick's High School;
3. Pupil Equity Funding Our Lady & St Patrick's High Learning Community: A Strength-Based Intervention to Promoting Resilience and Growth Mind-Set through Solution Oriented Approaches; and
4. Pupil Equity Funding St Peter the Apostle Learning Community: Using the Friends for Life CBT Programme to target pupils vulnerable at transition to secondary school.

Transitions 1 project

From the research evidence the WDPS surmised that there is a significant expressive vocabulary gap between children from the richest and poorest backgrounds by the time that children start primary schooling around the age of 5 years; indeed, the gap is around 18 months. Similarly, there are significant disparities between those from poorer and richer backgrounds when comparing the amount of hours that children are read to. This means that there are significant differences in both the number of words and also the quality of interaction to which children are exposed in their early, formative years. Further evidence was gleaned locally from three nurseries with above average SIMD confirming evidence of vocabulary delay. This was buttressed by national research evidence from the Effective Pre-school Primary and Secondary Education study (EPPSE)[8] that 'clearly demonstrated differences in children's experiences based on differing home circumstances and parental level of education' (WDPS, 2017: 5).

The WDPS intervened with 3 nurseries comprising 130 children. This intervention comprised two approaches i.e. reciprocal teaching as promoted by Oczkus (2010) and *Word Aware* (Parsons and Branagan, 2016). Their aim was to produce a coherent methodology for staff whereby increased attention was paid to the use of vocabulary. At the pre-intervention stage a snapshot was taken of pupils' vocabulary and during the intervention WDPS coached staff in the adoption of these two approaches. This resulted in post-intervention assessment which ascertained 'statistically significant improvement ... in vocabulary scores of taught words' (WDPS, 2017: 7). Clearly, a successful intervention underwritten by the WDPS and, in their 'lessons learned' section, are to be found several recommendations for future action – including the eye-catching 'Continue to mentor and support staff in providing high quality interactions through the use of VERP (video enhanced reflective practice)' (WDPS, 2017: 8).

Establishing multi-agency hubs project

The plan from West Dunbartonshire Council was to meet the increasing social and emotional needs of 'at-risk' young people by setting up 'multi-agency hubs' in Clydebank High School and Our Lady & St Patrick's High School, Dumbarton. A variety of additional support and tailored interventions were put in place. This was premised on their belief, derived from research, that 'supporting social and emotional learning can lead to improved attainment, particularly for at-risk groups such as looked-after children and children growing up in poverty' (WDPS, 2017:11).

The Educational Psychology Service identified three main areas for their specialised input i.e.:

- whole-school nurture approaches training;
- mindfulness; and
- de-escalation training for staff.

With regard to nurture – through their attendance at training events and visiting other schools, staff at Clydebank High School and Our Lady & St Patrick's High School swiftly came to the realisation of the benefits of a whole-school approach to nurture. From this approach staff identified 'a shared framework from which to enhance their understanding of child development and reflect on ... impact on learning and behaviour' (WDPS, 2017:12). With respect to mindfulness, school staff are to be trained to become Mindfulness practitioners themselves such that the perceived benefits of mindfulness (calmness, less anxiety) can be cascaded within the two high schools. At that point in time, de-escalation training for staff also lay in the future and West Dunbartonshire Council was seeking to buy in expertise from near neighbours, Glasgow City Council.

The other two projects, Promoting Resilience and Growth Mind-Set and Friends for Life CBT Programme were at similar, early stages of development when the Education Scotland inspection took place. However, with the amount of scoping, data collection and piloting undertaken it is clear to see why the inspectorate were confident about the ability of West Dunbartonshire Council to evaluate the impact of these initiatives. This confidence rests upon, primarily, the involvement of the Educational Psychology Service.[9] From a classroom perspective such a service is usually seen within the context of individualised assessment and support for troubled or gifted pupils; but from a strategic perspective the experience of West Dunbartonshire Council suggests that they have a wide-ranging role to perform in the support of initiatives combatting the poverty-related attainment gap.

The Renfrewshire Way

After trialling this new process with West Dunbartonshire Council, Education Scotland turned its attention to Renfrewshire Council which was to receive the accolade of being:

> the first local authority in Scotland to be rated 'excellent' for its progress in narrowing the attainment gap between pupils from deprived areas and their more affluent peers ... [indeed] Scotland's chief inspector of education has described the progress being made ... in closing the attainment gap as 'an absolute delight'.
>
> (Seith 2019)

Intrigued by this fulsome praise, I arranged a professional conversation with Steven Quinn, Director of Children's Services.

Monday, 10 June 2019
Renfrewshire Council HQ, Paisley

STEVEN: Well, the Renfrewshire Way ... the staff talk about it a lot ... I suppose the Renfrewshire Way for them would be now there is direction. There are parameters but there is freedom.

AL: Freedom within a structure.

STEVEN: To work within that structure. So, in other words if you get it right, you get all the praise in the world; if you get it wrong we'll support you (and I'll take that) and we'll keep working together. But we talk about support through challenge and our schools have taken that on board terrifically well. They actually have really engaged with it. We challenge our schools continually through our Quality Improvement Framework.

And a starting point for quality improvement is data:

STEVEN: I have a data analyst, not a statistician but a data analyst that I appointed through the Attainment Challenge. We know at any given stage the attainment, the attendance of every child in Renfrewshire at any given time. We can benchmark them against free meal entitlement, against footwear and clothing entitlement, about where they live, against their attendance, against the family of schools they're in, whatever. We do all the analysis centrally and then we use that to support the schools, we give them it.

At one level, these practices are quite common throughout the UK, but much depends upon *who* is doing the analysis and *how* they do it:

STEVEN: ... and that's one of the reasons I have within the team a project manager who's got no educational background in terms of schools. In terms of being a teacher. My data person doesn't come from a teaching ... my research people don't come from teaching but they bring a different eye to it ... and a different vision, a different lens, they understand critical indicators, they understand what's an outcome, they understand how to collect data and how to quantify it, and how to qualify it. And they're working with schools to support that journey because that's not an expertise necessarily that a head teacher has.

As with West Dunbartonshire's use of the Educational Psychology Service, there appear to be clear benefits in working alongside professionals from non-teaching backgrounds who have expertise and skills that are uncommon within the teaching profession. They have much to offer us:

STEVEN: Becoming better at understanding qualitative and quantitative data. I think we're very good at analysing quantitative data because we like that and its easy. Sixty per cent of kids, now 64%, that's better: 60, 62, 64, 66, 68, we're getting better. But you also have to look at qualitative data and we're really poor in education at collecting qualitative data.

And once collected then this data has to be presented and disseminated:

STEVEN: I brought one particular young woman in, incredible young woman; and we were doing case studies on the Pupil Equity Fund and Attainment Challenge work we were doing; and we had former head teachers just recently retired who were supporting us in this, going out and interviewing the heads and talking to them and gathering evidence, writing up a short report. She came and said, 'Nobody will read those reports.' I said, 'How do you know that?' 'Because they're bland, it's just writing ...' They were in Education Scotland formats. She said ... 'I'll write it up, can I go out with them?' 'Absolutely! On you go.' That's now throughout Scotland.

Her presentation of this work can be found in the 40-page document by Renfrewshire Council (2018) titled *Renfrewshire Attainment Challenge*. Addressing five areas of Learning and Teaching, Families and Communities, Leadership, Data Analysis and Pupil Equity Fund this booklet has a stated aim to:

> showcase innovative, evidence-based approaches and interventions which are being implemented across Renfrewshire schools. A range of case studies, evaluations and overviews are included which demonstrate improvements in learning and teaching, health and wellbeing and a reduction in the poverty-related attainment gap.
>
> (Renfrewshire Council 2018:2)

At this juncture, it can be stated that the document does fulfil its stated aim of 'showcasing' interventions that are evidence-based. The case studies and evaluations are a form of evidence but they do not meet the criteria for being considered as research. Suffice to say, though, this booklet offers several examples of working hypotheses that are worthy of consideration for future research.

Collaboration for collective impact

A recurring thread in this professional conversation with Renfrewshire Council's Director of Children's Services is that of collaboration – and it starts at the highest levels of the organisation:

STEVEN: I think, to be fair, we're getting better, there's a much better understanding and recognition now that this is society's problem. That's one of the things I like about Renfrewshire, we see this as this is the council's responsibility to improve attainment. The council's responsibility to close the poverty-related attainment gap. Not the schools'. Not the teachers'. Not mine; it is all of our responsibilities as a community.

And this collective responsibility is a hallmark of education within Renfrewshire as Steven Quinn explains in response to a hypothetical question about underachievement:

AL: So you take an example, like your ... say it's a primary school and you've decided that the boys in P4–5 are underachieving in comparison to boys in other schools, or girls in the same school, that would be a focus for the data?
STEVEN: That could be a focus and the P4s in numeracy over a trend are not performing as well why, by the end of P4? Or the end of P1, P7 whatever. It would be a trend; we can't do it on one year. So what is it that the school needs to do? What supports are required? What do you need from the Development Officers through the Attainment Challenge

Funding as they are? What support can I get you from other schools? Head teachers will no longer see themselves, and that's the Renfrewshire Way as well, head teachers are not head teachers solely of their school. Their primary focus is … their own school, they have a secondary focus of supporting all children in Renfrewshire because *they're senior officers of the council* [emphasis added].

This is strikingly reminiscent of the professional conversation with Lee Hessey, CEO of The Forge Trust. As I remarked:

AL: Well, that's where that Academy Trust … that's how Lee speaks, the way you've just spoken there. That we all sink and swim together. We are all in this, it's six schools and we're all in it, we're all helping each other. And if somebody's got a problem, we've all got a problem.

However, Steven Quinn strongly disavowed the competitive element of The Forge Trust's approach as he reflected, ruefully, upon his past experiences:

STEVEN: I think really, really effective schools work on that principle of getting to collective impact, that's that whole thing about … I'm embarrassed by it if I'm being honest; but you're thinking changes as you do different jobs in education and my thinking has changed incredibly over time. As a principal teacher … in fact as a class teacher there was almost a willingness for the kids in your class to do as well as they could, better than they did elsewhere … and you almost revelled in the Maths results being better than the English, or the Science, or whatever; and then as a head teacher you revelled in the fact that your school's results overall were better than the other schools in the STACS (Standards Tables and Charts) list, or the neighbouring schools … And I understand all of that; but the only way we're going to get real improvement in the system is where there's a will to work collectively across classrooms and a department, across departments in the school, across schools in an authority and across authorities.

The message coming across strongly is that of *collaboration for collective impact*. A question, though, is how is this created? The Director of Children's Services at Renfrewshire Council has little doubt that leadership is the key to creating such a culture of collective responsibility that motivates staff and promotes good pedagogy:

STEVEN: So it's about an ethos or a culture in the school rather than a teacher who invariably then gets promoted and leaves and has gone, it's about creating culture, creating ethos, creating an energy in the school rather than focusing on one particular teacher.
        Well, I think there are two things. I would argue that number one, the quality of the leadership in the school because a fantastic head will develop great teachers. So, number one above everything else is the quality of the leader in that school. To me, they create the culture, they create the ethos, they create the environment and they make ordinary teachers very good. They make very good teachers exceptional teachers. They bring everybody up a notch; and number two is the quality of learning and teaching in the classroom. If those two things are incredible, everything else can either happen or not happen. I suggest it will probably happen anyway.

... what you can do is you can create the climate and create the environment to allow people to find that spark that motivates them and that's what I would hope we're trying to do in Renfrewshire ... Create an environment, create a culture, create an ethos which allows people to find that spark that motivates them.

Evidence that all of this is being achieved is provided not only in their own report (Renfrewshire Council, 2018) and the Education Scotland (2019a) inspection but also by the frequency of visits from other local authorities – five at the time of our professional conversation – with one having taken place the previous working day:

STEVEN: Cumbria ... they had read our inspection report. I wasn't in on Friday, I was in Edinburgh. The team had organised the visit and one of the things that they said at the end of the day; they said we've spoken to head teachers, we've spoken to Education Managers, we've spoken to Development Officers; we've set up meetings with all and sundry. He said, 'No matter who we've spoken to today, every single person gives us the identical messages. You are in this together; nobody is more important than the next person and unless you get it right, we can't get it right.'

Again, the theme of *collaboration for collective impact* rears its head:

STEVEN: It's a very simple thing, we talk about it all the time in Renfrewshire now, where you've got ... what happens is people work with that. It's basically disorder and confusion, everybody is trying their hardest but they're all knocking against each other. And then you start to move to that which is probably individual impact, so we're kind of starting to really, at least know what we're trying to do. There's a way, there's a vision, there's a purpose but we're all going at it in a different direction and then you get to a sort of coordinated impact which is that sort of thing (using diagram).

AL: Some are further along than others?

STEVEN: Yeah. But see when you get there ... the collective impact, then you're really motoring because everything is pushing everything along. Everybody is doing work with the same approach but, collectively, and all of a sudden you get real 'buy in'. So, when we look at our transition, for example, from P7 into S1 – we ensure our Numeracy Development Officer is working along with the Literacy Development Officer, along with the Health & Wellbeing Officer, along with our Transitions Officer; because it's no longer about a pastoral transition. It's a curriculum transition; but we're working in partnership with parents, so everybody is in this together and then, who do we need to support most? Who are our most vulnerable and are going to struggle in this transition? And how do we ensure that we put the supports in for them? And we move the teacher with them – from primary into secondary – for three months to support those kids along that journey. That idea of coordinated and collective impact rather than everybody doing their own wee bit; and that takes time to get there.

This notion of *collaboration for collective impact* sits well with the national consciousness of Scotland. Throughout my lifetime the populace has consistently returned left-of-centre parties, the Labour Party and the Scottish National Party (SNP) to seats of government – be it Westminster or Holyrood.[10] Indeed, Her Majesty's Chief Inspector of Education (HMCIE) in

Scotland, Gayle Gorman, commented to *TES Scotland* that, in comparison with our southern neighbours: 'We [in Scotland] fundamentally have a different societal focus around education. We believe in equity and opportunity for all our young people, and our education system really reflects that' (Hepburn, 2018). And that struck a discordant note. Aren't Lee Hessey and The Forge Trust all about equity and opportunity for their pupils? One would struggle to find a more left-wing upbringing than Lee's. And what about Wendy Morton and the Ad Astra Primary Partnership – weren't those staff and head teachers – Helen Chambers, Jo Cook, Peter Stonier, Chris Wilson and Grant Worthington – weren't they all driven by a desire to achieve 'equity and opportunity' for their children (Luby, 2019)? And did not their education system of academies, Trusts, teaching schools and research schools enable and support the fulfilment of their desire?

There is a sense abroad in Scotland that we have a more community-oriented approach as affirmed by our comprehensive system of education. As teachers we can point to the General Teaching Council Scotland (GTCS) Standards that place 'social justice' at the heart of the Professional Values and Personal Commitment core to being a teacher.[11] But maybe it is not quite that simple. It seems that, on the surface, Scotland can lay greater claim to a community-based system of education supported by all political parties, not just left-of-centre. England's system is more fragmented with free schools, academies, comprehensives, etc. This would suggest that Steven Quinn's concept of *coordinated and collective impact* is more straightforward to achieve in Scotland. However, there are strong similarities in the professional conversations north and south of the border about *social justice* and also *aspiration* and *humility*.

Aspiration

My initial contacts with the Ad Astra Primary Partnership quickly revealed a set of head teachers united by a common bond of 'no excuses'. Quite simply, no excuses would be accepted for not promoting, encouraging and developing the interests and aptitudes of their children. Indeed, they compared the educational opportunities of their pupils with those who attend independent schools. They saw no reason that, as far as possible, similar opportunities would not be afforded to their children. The head teachers are not naïve. They know that in terms of resources, financial and physical, they are unlikely to ever match the fee-paying independent schools. However, with respect to the most important resource – *teachers* – Chris, Grant, Helen, Jo and Lee all believe that they are better placed than the independent sector.

Such confidence fuels their belief in high aspirations from their staff, their pupils and the parents of their pupils. And the second statement from Steven Quinn in our professional conversation tells a similar story, namely:

STEVEN: Auchenlodment in Johnstone. I'll blindfold you, take you on a car journey and take you into these schools. I defy you to tell me you're in some of the toughest areas in Renfrewshire. You'll think you're in a leafy suburb because of the expectation, the way the children speak in that school, the way they conduct themselves, the way the school presents itself; everything about that school exudes ambition, aspiration, expectation.

This is strongly reminiscent of the research case studies undertaken for the Ad Astra Primary Partnership (Luby, 2016) whose schools are sited within the top deciles for deprivation. Further, as outlined in the previous chapter, the Ad Astra Primary Partnership addresses five issues of poverty, two of which are directly relevant i.e. poverty of language and poverty of aspiration. The qualities praised by Renfrewshire's Director of Children's Services are achieved through *coordinated and collective impact* at a regional level; whilst similar qualities are praised by Ofsted (2018) for an East Midlands school that would also lay claim to a coordinated, collective approach at the level of a Multi-Academy Trust.

And there's more ...

Humility

Another noticeable feature of the Ad Astra heads is their humility. They are not without ego: but they continually think of others and how they can better be of help to them - pupils and staff. And this character trait is not confined within specific geographical borders:

STEVEN: If you asked the head teacher, Gerry Carlton to rate himself on a scale of 1 to 10, he would probably say 4 or 5. My view would be 10. Not 9, 10. Similarly I've got other head teachers identical - Jackie, Emma, Lynne, et cetera, et cetera, right. But one of the things, for a lot of them, that makes them so good is - they don't think they are ...

AL: ...what you said there about head teachers. I'm thinking of Helen Chambers who's very self-effacing; and she's done a wonderful job in a very difficult mining village in the East Midlands. She encapsulates what you said, she just doesn't realise how good she is. Even when you tell her, she won't accept it. She can't believe she's exceptional.

STEVEN: Do you know the only way I think they do accept it, even privately, is when they also get the opportunity to visit other schools and support the Quality Improvement Framework that we have here, or other authorities have; and they then go into these schools and, even privately, they're thinking to themselves ... they don't do this, they don't do that. Why are they not doing this? Why are they not doing that? ...

Why not? Let's change it or let's analyse it at least and say we can make it work better for that child, those children, those families.

There is much in common to be found amongst teaching staff on both sides of the border. A coordinated and collective impact can improve pupils' learning when organised strategically at regional level, or locally, at Trust level. The education systems in Scotland and England *are* different - but the people? From my experience, those endeavouring to close the poverty-related attainment gap share the virtue of humility - in its Catholic sense i.e. people knowing themselves as they truly are. They know the reality of the situation which they face and the challenges that it presents; and they are willing to seek the help of others for a remedy.

From this examination of Caledonia and the Scottish Attainment Challenge we learn of the successes of the local councils of Glasgow City, Renfrewshire and West Dunbartonshire - and a recurrent theme of *collaboration for collective impact*. The successes engendered by these councils run counter to the claim of McCluskey (2017: 32, emphasis added) that 'Efforts to close the gap in attainment ... [and] to address the central problem of the link between poverty and attainment, have had too little impact thus far in many countries, *including Scotland.*'

Let us return south of the border and look at their endeavours to close the poverty-related attainment gap through coordinated and collective impact – particularly as envisaged through two of the Ad Astra partnership schools.

Notes

1 See www.roughguides.com/gallery/most-beautiful-country-in-the-world/
2 Education Scotland is an executive agency of the Scottish Government tasked with improving the quality of the country's education system. Created in 2010, it brought together the responsibilities of Her Majesty's Inspectorate of Education and Learning and Teaching Scotland which was an advisory body to the Scottish Government.
3 See www.glasgow.gov.uk/CHttpHandler.ashx?id=41724&p=0
4 In 2018-2019, the funding allocated to Glasgow City Council from the Attainment Scotland Fund was approx. £8 million, and just under £21.8 million from the Pupil Equity Fund. Taken together, this equates to approx. 6% of Glasgow City Council's total education budget.
5 See www.glasgow.gov.uk/index.aspx?articleid=23800
6 For further information, see GTCS (2012).
7 The 1888 'World Championship' took place in Glasgow on 19 May between the winners of the Scottish FA Cup, Renton, and the English FA Cup, West Bromwich Albion (WBA). Renton beat WBA by four goals to one.
8 For further information see www.ucl.ac.uk/ioe/research-projects/2019/mar/effective-pre-school-primary-and-secondary-education-project-eppse
9 Second, there is well-researched, peer-reviewed evidence from a Scottish context (Brown et al., 2012; Fernie and Cubeddu, 2016) furnishing support for the efficacy of *Working on What Works* which underpins the *Promoting Resilience and Growth Mind-Set* project.
10 A caveat is necessary in that in their early years the SNP were sometimes dubbed as the 'Tartan Tories'.
11 See www.gtcs.org.uk/web/files/the-standards/standards-for-registration-1212.pdf

References

Brown, E. L., Powell, E. and Clark, A. 2012. Working on What Works: working with teachers to improve classroom behaviour and relationships. *Educational Psychology in Practice: Theory, Research and Practice in Educational Psychology* 28(1) 19-30.

Education Scotland. 2018. [Online] *Inspection of local authorities. How well is West Dunbartonshire Council improving learning, raising attainment and closing the poverty-related attainment gap?* May 2018. Available from: https://education.gov.scot/media/q0xjmpr1/westdunbartonshirecouncilins010518.pdf [Accessed 22 April 2020]

Education Scotland. 2019a. [Online] *Inspection of local authorities. How well is Renfrewshire Council improving learning, raising attainment and closing the poverty-related attainment gap?* February 2019. Available from: https://blogs.glowscotland.org.uk/re/stjames/files/2019/03/Renfrewshire-Council-Childrens-Services-Report.pdf [Accessed 1 August 2019]

Education Scotland. 2019b. [Online] *Inspection of local authorities. How well is Glasgow City Council improving learning, raising attainment and closing the poverty-related attainment gap?* March 2019. Available from: https://education.gov.scot/media/wwhh2pd4/glasgowlains110319.pdf [Accessed 22 April 2020]

Fernie, L. and Cubeddu, D. 2016. WOWW: a solution orientated approach to enhance classroom relationships and behaviour within a Primary three class. *Educational Psychology in Practice: Theory, Research and Practice in Educational Psychology* 32(2) 197-208.

George, M. 2019. [Online] Reporter's take: what will Williamson do for schools? *Times Education Supplement.* 1 August 2019. Available from: www.tes.com/news/reporters-take-what-will-williamson-do-schools [Accessed 1 August 2019]

GTCS (General Teaching Council Scotland). 2012. [Online] *The Standard for Career-Long Professional Learning: supporting the development of teacher professional learning.* December 2012. Available from: www.gtcs.org.uk/web/FILES/the-standards/standard-for-career-long-professional-learning-1212.pdf [Accessed 1 August 2019]

Hepburn, H. 2018. [Online] Inspection body 'closer than ever to teachers'. *Times Education Supplement*. 10 December 2018. Available from: www.tes.com/news/inspection-body-closer-ever-teachers [Accessed 7 August 2019]

Hepburn, H. 2019. [Online] Children's education in Glasgow rated outstanding. *Times Education Supplement*. 11 March 2019. Available from: www.tes.com/news/childrens-education-glasgow-rated-outstanding [Accessed 30 July 2019]

Luby, A. 2016. *Poverty and Closing the Gap: Ad Astra Research Consultancy Projects*. Lincoln: Bishop Grosseteste University.

Luby, A. 2019. To the stars: Ad Astra addressing poverty. In P. Beckley (Ed.) *Supporting Vulnerable Children in Early Years: Practical Guidance and Strategies for Working with Children at Risk*. London: Jessica Kingsley.

McCluskey, G. 2017. Closing the attainment gap in Scottish schools: three challenges in an unequal society. *Education, Citizenship and Social Justice* 12(1) 24–35.

Oczkus, L. 2010. *Reciprocal Teaching at Work K-12: Powerful Strategies and Lessons for Improving Reading Comprehension*. Newark, DE: International Reading Association.

OECD. 2015. [Online] *Improving schools in Scotland: an OECD perspective*. Available from: www.oecd.org/education/school/Improving-Schools-in-Scotland-An-OECD-Perspective.pdf [Accessed 30 July 2019]

Ofsted. 2018. [Online] *Short inspection: The Sir Donald Bailey Academy*. March 2018. Available from: https://files.api.ofsted.gov.uk/v1/file/2762679 [Accessed 8 August 2019]

Parsons, S. and Branagan, A. 2016. *Word Aware 2: Teaching Vocabulary in the Early Years*. London: Speechmark Publishing Ltd.

Paterson, L. 2018. [Online] *Scotland's Curriculum for Excellence: the betrayal of a whole generation?* Available from: http://eprints.lse.ac.uk/88472/1/politicsandpolicy-curriculum-for.pdf [Accessed 30 July 2019]

Renfrewshire Council. 2018. *Renfrewshire Attainment Challenge*. August 2018. Paisley: Renfrewshire Council.

Seith, E. 2019. [Online] Inspectorate 'delighted' with council closing attainment gap. *Times Education Supplement*. 19 February 2019. Available from: www.tes.com/news/inspectorate-delighted-council-closing-attainment-gap [Accessed 7 August 2019]

Silvester, N. 2018. [Online] New study reveals shocking extent of poverty and deprivation in neglected parts of Scotland. *Daily Record*. Available from: www.dailyrecord.co.uk/news/scottish-news/shock-figures-reveal-over-half-12916659 [Accessed 29 July 2019]

WDPS (West Dunbartonshire Psychological Service). 2017. [Online] *Progress made in improving learning, raising attainment and closing the poverty related attainment gap through projects funded by the Scottish Attainment Challenge and Pupil Equity Fund*. November 2017. Available from: Principal Educational Psychologist, Psychological Services, c/o Carleith Primary School, Stark Avenue, Duntocher, Clydebank, G81 6EF.

3 East Midlands and beyond

... a cosy pub tucked into the corner of an almost quintessential English village in Sherwood Forest. Here, I enjoyed the company of Wendy Morton, an experienced and accomplished educationist in the realm of school improvement. Wendy is a driving force in establishing the Ad Astra Primary Partnership that comprises ...

> six founder schools [that] share the same challenge ... of increasing progression and narrowing the attainment gap for predominantly 'white British working class pupils in areas of deprivation'.

(Luby 2019: 33)

In the early summer of 2016 I had my first in-depth conversation with Wendy Morton who, helpfully, set the context for the birth of this partnership. Highly experienced within school improvement services, Wendy had become concerned with simplistic approaches to 'closing the gap'. In particular, since 2010 Free School Meals (FSM) had been used as a proxy indicator of poverty but this was regarded by many as being too limited and simplistic. In order to address the complexity of the situation, Wendy cross-referenced the influential 2014 House of Commons Select Committee report, *Underachievement in education by white working class children* with the Rowntree report published in the same year, *Monitoring poverty and social exclusion*. She then convened a meeting of six like-minded primary school head teachers whom she thought could collaborate with each other. Prior to their first meeting each head teacher had to read the Commons report and, at the meeting, there was no agenda in order to prompt free-flowing discussion. Likewise, The Sir Donald Bailey Academy hosted the next session and, again, there was no agenda. The group enjoyed 'breathing space' such that they could freely exchange ideas and information.

The head teachers were adopting an interpretative approach to educational practice (see Figure 3.1) by not only considering the objective evidence furnished by the House of Commons and the Rowntree Commons reports; but also their own subjective experiences came into play. As indicated below, they were communicating through the exchange of information, ideas and feelings. Above all, their deliberations were moral: what *ought* we to do in this situation of trying to close the poverty related attainment gap?

From their discussions a broad agreement emerged from the head teachers around a theme of 'White British Working Class in Areas of Underachievement'. Further, their sense of identity was strengthened by adopting the name Ad Astra (To the stars). Similarly, a sense

Form: *Interpretative* - the form of knowledge of educational practice is interpretative i.e. being concerned with explaining the meaning of said practice it seeks to use both subjective and objective evidence.

Nature: *Communicative* - educational practice is held to be essentially communicative in nature i.e. it is concerned with the exchanging of information, ideas and feelings.

Function: *Practical* - the function of teachers is practical, in that they consider said informed explanations of educational practice as a basis for their deliberations about what ought to be done in a particular situation.

Figure 3.1 Interpretative approach to educational practice
Source: adapted from Carr (1986)

of commitment was engendered through the writing up of a Memorandum of Understanding that was signed by all of the head teachers. The focus of the Ad Astra Primary Partnership was enhanced through its development of 'Perspectives of Poverty' and its five strands of Material, Emotional, Language, Experience and Aspiration. Shortly thereafter, a supportive letter from Her Majesty's Inspectorate in England approved their good practices and the Ad Astra partnership was up and running.

I was invited to attend the next meeting of the Ad Astra partnership of which an integral feature was the socialising over lunch; and this eased my entry into this community of school leaders. Their contribution was to be not only sandwiches and cups of tea; but also insight into the practices and ideals of school staff committed to alleviating the effects of poverty upon their children. It soon became apparent that my contribution would be to undertake research consultancy projects with several of the Ad Astra schools.

Mansfield against poverty

The first research project was undertaken five miles south-west of Mansfield in the small town of Kirkby in Ashfield formerly renowned for mining and railways. The local schools serve an area of very high social and economic disadvantage and the Ad Astra school, Abbey Hill Primary and Nursery School, has almost half of their pupils living in families that are income deprived.[1] The school does receive substantial pupil premium funding but other indices of deprivation show that education, skills and training are significantly low in the local area. This poverty is further demonstrated by a number of families receiving support from social services and the school employs Sam – a full-time Child and Family Support Worker. It is not uncommon for the self-effacing head teacher, Helen Chambers, to accompany Sam on her 'rounds' to awaken and cajole some of their charges to attend school.

Prior to visiting the school, I was aware that the school was rated 'Good' by Ofsted but that it faced challenges. As the Ofsted (2014: 4) inspection report comments: 'The children join the Nursery with skills and knowledge that are well below those typically found. They are particularly low in speaking and listening and in reading and writing.' Through professional conversations with Abbey Hill staff it became apparent that they were particularly energised to address the development of handwriting skills (Ad Astra strand of poverty of language). This was evidenced by comments from staff in Pre-school, Nursery and Years 1 and 2 e.g.:

- 'Been on the agenda for the last few years.'
- 'Data from boys' handwriting has been a prompt; topic has been discussed before, performance targets; school plan ...'
- 'Foundation reports generally show weakness with respect to handwriting skills.'
- 'Starting from a very low base. Tracking 2 year olds from Nottinghamshire Council showed children at a significant risk of delay.'
- 'There are long-term handwriting problems.'

(Luby, 2019:36)

One member of staff who had moved to the area from a comparable, working class area, could not help but draw an unfavourable comparison that 'there is a noticeable difference in (physical) development of the pupils'. Other staff, who had made a similar move, made similar comments such as:

- a physical lack of development, curved backs from pushchairs;
- heads too large in comparison with their bodies with a lack of balance e.g. head tilting forward; and
- poor language development e.g. unable to utter broken sentences or, indeed, even single words.

(Luby 2016:6)

The recent opening of the Pre-school for the arrival of 2 year olds had triggered an emphasis on teacher professional development and this led to a 'knowledge explosion' amongst the staff. Much of this new understanding was attributed to in-service training provided by a specialist, Paul Young, that they described as 'informative' and 'amazing'. This had induced a greater awareness and understanding amongst staff of underlying problems with regard to a lack of development in children's handwriting skills. That such in-service training had a positive impact carries import as the type of professional development for teachers regarding handwriting development 'can have significant impacts on children's writing that can endure for at least 2 years' (Jones and Christensen, 2012:223). Generally, staff cited becoming more aware of the links between physical development and handwriting skills such as:

- visual clues for lack of gross motor and fine motor skills;
- tripod grip is an example of fine motor skills but whole hand grip is gross motor and use of the latter indicates a lack of the former;
- beanbag brain exercising game;
- importance of crawling for proper development of balance; and
- story conventions are necessary and that for literacy, physical skill is required.

(Luby 2016:6-7)

Such development of understanding amongst teaching staff and teaching assistants is commendable. Indeed, it is particularly significant since according to a highly authoritative volume of work,[2] 'Most studies of children's handwriting acquisition focused on the elementary school years, and there is scarce information about the development of writing skills before that time' (Vilageliu et al., 2012:7). This suggests that Abbey Hill school is of interest to the wider world of education. Partial confirmation is derived from a subsequent Ofsted (2018a) short inspection report that comments 'the school has demonstrated strong practice and marked improvement in specific areas'. In particular, Ofsted (2018a) draw attention to 'a display of pupils' writing [that] starts with mark-making by two-year-olds and shows how skills are developed as pupils progress through the school, finishing with examples of high-quality writing by the oldest pupils, all beautifully presented'.[3]

For me, the most compelling features of this research consultancy project are four-fold. First, the humility of head teacher, Helen Chambers. As per the discussion with Steven Quinn in the previous chapter – good leaders are endowed with humility – a humility that is founded on realism. Helen is well aware of the challenges confronting her school. This ranges from variable ratings of 'satisfactory' and 'requires improvement' from Ofsted (2011, 2012) to dissenting 'voices in the playground'. The school has won an award for parental engagement and one of the dissenting voices now appears in a You-Tube segment praising the work of the school! I have invited Helen into university to address newly qualified teachers on a course and, like them, I have listened and watched attentively, nay enchanted, as she talks of Abbey Hill school life. I have witnessed her in full presentation mode as she 'blows away' the delegates at a regional conference, 'Evidence-based Approaches to Closing the Gap'.[4] But Helen does not see herself as special, different, blessed. I do. Why is this?

AL: No, I saw that myself with the likes of Helen, that Helen doesn't ... either fails to recognise or just is so humble, doesn't realise how good she is and the impact she's making.

WENDY MORTON: I think when you're in it every day it's second nature, it's what you do; and therefore you don't see what other people do, heads don't visit each other's schools. They don't see what other people do, all they get is told what they do; and one of the things Ad Astra enabled people to do was to go and see each other's schools.[5] That was sometimes just to talk, it wasn't anything significant but sometimes out of that came ... it's the little things that make the difference ...

    ... and it's always been the case, you need facilitators ... I hate that word but facilitation is an art and it's about persuasion, knowledge, mobilisation of what people can do and also not taking the credit yourself. They take the credit. They've done the work. They're just not very good at knowing what they've done sometimes.

And this introduces the second of the four-fold features – the quiet leadership skills of 'facilitation'. A facilitation that is not passive but active with regard to 'persuading, knowing and mobilising'. It is the art of 'taking people with you'. This fosters respect – the kind of respect evident in the professional conversations with staff at Helen's school. And these staff exhibit a third feature – a quiet determination. There is no 'shouting from the rooftops' – rather there is an undercurrent of a steely determination to provide the best for the pupils in their care.

Finally, the school staff have developed a greater awareness of the influence of home background on children's lack of development in handwriting skills e.g.:

- lack of access to basics such as pens and paper;
- lack of encouragement at home;

- lack of literacy at home; and
- the overall, deleterious effects of this technological age exemplified by simple but crucial deficiencies such as wrong grip from pupils.

But more impressive than their growing awareness of the problems is their knowledge of practical solutions. For instance, within their first 15 hours at the Nursery the children have a progress check that establishes a baseline through tracking tools such as Primary ECaT (Every Child a Talker). Abbey Hill school members of staff implement a variety of activities and practices to enable the children to make good progress e.g.:

- encouraging use of basic mark-making i.e. blank paper on easel and children mark-make independently;
- reducing availability of tablets as they are a 'draw' for children but they impair development of keyboarding skills;
- undertaking 10-minute daily activities such as 'bean-bags'; and
- using Storyteller with props to engage children and painting activities to help to develop gross motor skills.

(Luby 2016:7)

From such activities, the staff are forming professional judgements that some progress in the development of handwriting skills is being established; citing evidences such as children displaying enjoyment of writing by spending time mark-making and less time on construction toys. And, as might be expected, Abbey Hill's successes are not confined to handwriting. As outlined above, a strength is parental engagement which is developed through a series of planned activities e.g.:

- Christmas Crafts which has … seen more parents coming in to the school and taking an interest and socialising with children and other parents;
- Keepsake Box for school-based items that are of interest and/or use at home;
- Parent & Toddler group that will use 'drop-ins' to increase parental awareness of handwriting skills and other activities;
- Munch 'n Mingle … [to] heighten parental awareness of the availability of simple, cheap yet healthy snacks; and
- Grandparents' Day … [to] include an art based 'family tree' activity and a writing based task.

(Luby 2016:8)

In addressing the poverty-related attainment gap, Abbey Hill has a wealth of ideas and practices.[6] Moreover, it evidences Dylan Wiliam's (TES, 2016) claim that 'professional development needs to focus on changing practice'.

It became clear that when Helen consulted her staff they were not slow in coming forward with ideas. The manner in which the ideas were harnessed and taken forward suggests that they were being given sufficient time and support to implement new ideas and practices. Similar discoveries were to be made with the next research consultancy project following a 5-mile road journey south-west to the most westerly point of Nottinghamshire at the border with Derbyshire.

Amber Valley against poverty

Jacksdale is a small, former mining village with a population of just over 3,000 as recorded at the last national census. At that time, there were 250 pupils in the school including a number of children on roll from Amber Valley which is in the top 10% most deprived areas nationally. A quarter of the children are entitled to pupil premium funding and the school was judged as 'Good' following its Ofsted (2015) inspection – a judgement subsequently confirmed in a further short inspection report (Ofsted, 2018b). The research at Jacksdale comprised a series of 45-minute professional conversations with 8 members of the teaching staff; and the co-researcher had a further exploratory meeting with the head teacher.

The exploratory meeting between the head teacher and the co-researcher, an experienced, former head teacher herself, helps to set the context. It was clear from the 'on entry' data in the Nursery school that children arrive with very weak communication skills. The school staff suspect that parent-child communication is being weakened through the prolonged use of dummies; and that i-pads, or similar devices, are being used to keep children quiet. It is noticeable that such issues affect whole cohorts of children and not just groups. Further, the school staff believes that the children are lacking in experiences and this inhibits language development. A further consequence of weak communication skills and low parental input is historically low Year 1 phonics check results (c. 43%). However, the introduction of *Read, Write, Inc.* has witnessed a dramatic rise to 88%. The school staff believe that this rise is due to the greater emphasis that *Read, Write, Inc.* places on reading aloud. Indeed, reading aloud is the element which the staff believe to have had the greatest impact on attainment and progress in this area.

However, the Jacksdale innovation that most intrigued fellow members of the Ad Astra Primary Partnership was their use of 'Marvellous Me' – a web-based application (app) that allows adults in school to send 'good news' messages directly to the phones of parents and carers. The intention is not only to get them more interested in what their children are learning, but also to encourage them to talk with their children about what they have been doing at school. Therefore, messages such as, 'Ask Freddie about his science experiment today' are being sent home. The app sends back a 'Hi 5' to the school to show that parents have received the message. Jacksdale school reports that this has been highly effective and that they receive thousands of 'Hi 5s' over the year.

School-based research findings

At that time, I was still developing what I understood by a 'professional conversation' and for the Jacksdale staff it was, basically, a semi-structured interview focusing on four research questions.

For the first research question, I discussed with the staff which two or three of the nine criteria identified under the heading of 'What does poverty of language mean to us?' (Jacksdale, 2015) held most significance – and why?

The staff are adamant that the most significant criterion is that of *lack of language experience*. In their view, many of the children do not sufficiently experience the reading of stories at home; neither reading independently nor being encouraged by parents. Further, with regard to reading homework, some of the reading organisers are returned 'empty' on a regular basis. Akin to Abbey Hill, other factors include a lack of learning traditional nursery rhymes. Of most significance, perhaps, is the comment that when children are asked 'What did you do at the weekend? Christmas?' – this often elicits a response of 'Just played with X-box.' This detrimental impact of technology links with other aspects such as poverty of experience and poverty of aspiration. Another manifestation of lack of language experience is that some of the children are unused to questioning. Many of the staff report that they have to check for understanding through children's body language. In a small number of worrying cases there are children who are rude to their parents and ignore maxims such as 'Treat others as you would like to be treated' and 'Respect elders'.

The second most significant criterion is that of 'manners'. In this case, though, the staff believe that 'We're starting to get a handle on it' as affirmed by comments such as 'manners are definitely, massively improving'. This improvement is caused by the consistency of staff modelling, demonstrations and reinforcement. The teachers are quite firm with their pupils being prepared to interrupt inappropriate behaviour and to ban repeated use of innocuous but irritating words e.g. 'What?' This is replaced with 'Pardon' and the children correct their peers. Evidence for the success of these strategies is afforded by Ofsted (2015:1) who record that: 'Pupils are extremely polite and well behaved in lessons and around school. They play and work together harmoniously and are proud of their school.'

The second research topic identified other successful strategies employed by Jacksdale school e.g.:

- whole school 'Speak Out' competition;
- Speech & Language therapy being accessed;
- workshops – Surestart;
- Time 2 Talk 1-1; and
- nature walks and talks – National Trust membership.

According to staff the most beneficial activity was Time 2 Talk 1-1. Some noted that it caused them to spend more time thinking about the needs of the children and listening more to them. Overall, there was a conscious effort to deliberately make time for their pupils even during breaks and snack-times. The staff believe that this effort is rewarded as it produces more contributions from the children. Also, the teachers affirm that children's behaviour seems to be improving as they voice their feelings even if, sometimes, they have to write it down first. Further, there is improved feedback from children with more 'child-speak' taking place within teacher-pupil conversations.

Appreciative inquiry

This positive experience raises an interesting consideration with respect to research. In the world of education research the method of appreciative inquiry is (pun intended) little appreciated. It is similar to action research as both share an emphasis on research for change, developing knowledge through an exploration of current practice, and an application of findings to inform strategies for the future (Reed et al., 2009). However, appreciative inquiry is distinct in that it focuses on positive aspects of practice rather than problems. For example, at Jacksdale school the teachers adopt different approaches to Time 2 Talk 1-1. One teacher uses an informal approach to selecting one or two pupils during registration; and then spends the 20 minutes' time allocation for an in-depth chat – often in the corridor. Whilst this is taking place, other pupils are doing different 'morning jobs' with a teaching assistant present in the classroom. Two other members of the teaching staff, though, employ the strategy of 'Puppet & Puppeteer' in paired conversations at registration with the topics being set by the teacher. Given that the teachers were unaware of these differences in practice, then this contrast of approaches may offer the school an opportunity to develop its 'understanding of evidence-based teaching' (Hammersley-Fletcher et al., 2015: 23). Through the use of appreciative inquiry, it could prove interesting to research, compare and analyse these contrasting uses of Time 2 talk 1-1.

Certainly, in my experience, when a school considers undertaking research into activities within its own premises it tends to focus on issues that are problematic; and this may prove to be daunting. It is never easy to address one's own weaknesses – particularly if one is uncertain as to the helpfulness of the methods used to gather evidence. Are they appropriate? Relevant? Valid? Faced with such considerations it seems preferable to consider an area of strength. What are we good at? It is an easier task to seek evidence when one already believes that the findings will be positive and plentiful.

Just beyond the East Midlands – in a South Yorkshire metropolitan borough – is to be found a school that is comfortable with research and well versed in evidence-based practices. Let us pay them a visit.

Notes

1   As indicated by the school's score on the Income Deprivation Affecting Children Index.
2   This volume is 'an overview of a large number of research programmes spread across 15 European countries' (Torrance, 2012: xxix)
3   The most recent Ofsted (2019) report indicates that the school 'requires improvement' but this is undoubtedly due to the unfortunate, long-term absence of the head teacher.
4   Evidence-based Approaches to Closing the Gap, regional conference, Bishop Grosseteste University, Lincoln, June 2016.
5   This invites comparison with Steven Quinn's comments in the previous chapter and highlights the desirability of head teachers visiting others' schools.
6   Further examples can be found in Luby (2016: 12-16).

References

Carr, W. 1986. Theories of theory and practice. *Journal of Philosophy of Education* 20(2) 177-186.
Hammersley-Fletcher, L., Lewin, C., Davies, C., Duggan, J., Rowley, H. and Spink, E. 2015. [Online] *Evidence-based teaching: advancing capability and capacity for enquiry in schools. Interim report.* National College for Teaching and Leadership. Available from: https://assets.publishing.service.gov. uk/government/uploads/system/uploads/attachment_data/file/464596/EBT_Interim_report_FINAL. pdf [Accessed 24 August 2019]
House of Commons Select Committee. 2014. [Online] *Underachievement in education by white working class children.* June 2014. London: The Stationery Office. Available from: https://publications.parlia- ment.uk/pa/cm201415/cmselect/cmeduc/142/142.pdf [Accessed 21 August 2019]
Jacksdale. 2015. *Exploring the concepts of 'Poverty' and 'Spoken Language' at Jacksdale Primary School.* Nottinghamshire: Jacksdale Nursery and Primary School.
Jones, D. and Christensen, C. A. 2012. Impact of teacher professional development in handwriting on improved student learning outcomes in writing quality. In M. Fayol et al. (Eds) *Translation of Thought*

to Written Text While Composing: Advancing Theory, Knowledge, Research Methods, Tools, and Applications. New York: Taylor & Francis.

Luby, A. 2016. *Poverty and Closing the Gap: Ad Astra Research Consultancy Projects.* Lincoln: Bishop Grosseteste University.

Luby, A. 2019. To the stars: Ad Astra addressing poverty. In P. Beckley (Ed.) *Supporting Vulnerable Children in the Early Years: Practical Guidance and Strategies for Working with Children at Risk.* London: Jessica Kingsley Publishers.

Ofsted. 2011. [Online] *School inspection report: Abbey Hill Primary & Nursery.* Unique Reference Number (URN):136006. 12–13 May 2011. Available from: https://files.api.ofsted.gov.uk/v1/file/1972865 [Accessed 22 August 2019]

Ofsted. 2012. [Online] *School inspection report: Abbey Hill Primary & Nursery.* 31 October–1 November 2012. Available from: https://files.api.ofsted.gov.uk/v1/file/2109475 [Accessed 22 August 2019]

Ofsted. 2014. [Online] *School inspection report: Abbey Hill Primary & Nursery.* 25 February 2014. Available from: https://files.api.ofsted.gov.uk/v1/file/2350165 [Accessed 21 August 2019]

Ofsted. 2015. [Online] *School inspection report: Jacksdale Primary and Nursery School.* 11–12 February 2015. URN: 122580. Available from: https://files.api.ofsted.gov.uk/v1/file/2459833 [Accessed 22 August 2019]

Ofsted. 2018a. [Online] *Short inspection report: Abbey Hill Primary & Nursery School.* 28 June 2018. Available from: https://files.api.ofsted.gov.uk/v1/file/2786587 [Accessed 22 August 2019]

Ofsted. 2018b. [Online] *Short inspection of Jacksdale Primary and Nursery School.* 21 November 2018. Available from: https://files.api.ofsted.gov.uk/v1/file/50045083 [Accessed 22 August 2019]

Ofsted. 2019. [Online] *School inspection report: Abbey Hill Primary & Nursery.* 10 July 2019. Available from: https://files.api.ofsted.gov.uk/v1/file/50091907 [Accessed 22 August 2019]

Reed, J., Nilsson, A. and Holmberg, L. 2009. Appreciative inquiry: research for action. In A. Dwivedi (Ed.) *Handbook of Research on Information Technology Management and Clinical Data Administration in Healthcare.* London: IGI Global.

Rowntree Report. 2014. [Online] *Monitoring poverty and social exclusion.* November 2014. Available from: www.jrf.org.uk/report/monitoring-poverty-and-social-exclusion-2014 [Accessed 21 August 2019]

TES editorial team. 2016. [Online] The 33 books every teacher should read. *Times Educational Supplement.* 5 January 2016. Available from: www.tes.com/news/school-news/ breaking-views/33-books-every-teacher-should-read [subscription required for access]

Torrance, M. 2012. Introduction: why we need writing research. In M. Torrance, D. Alamargot, M. Castello, F. Ganier, O. Kruse, A. Mangen, L. Tolchinsky and L. van Waes (Eds) *Learning to Write Effectively: Current Trends in European Research.* Bingley, Yorks: Emerald.

Vilageliu O. S., Kandel, S. and Aznar, M. A. 2012. Early development of handwriting motor skills. In M. Torrance et al. (Eds) *Learning to Write Effectively: Current Trends in European Research.* Bingley, Yorks: Emerald.

4 Pilgrims' progress through evidence-based practices

Introduction

A recent research briefing from the Education Endowment Foundation/National Foundation for Educational Research suggests that 'a number of research studies have shown that positive school cultures, in which teachers are encouraged and trusted to collaborate, investigate, experiment and take informed risks are often correlated with high levels of research engagement' (Walker et al., 2019: 4). Thankfully, I know such a school: it is Bawtry Mayflower primary and it is situated in the Metropolitan Borough of Doncaster in South Yorkshire. And, I know of others too.

First of all, though: *What is evidence? What counts as evidence? Who determines these?*

The simple answer is – or ought to be – 'Teachers' according to the 'father of teacher-research'. This accolade was earned by Lawrence Stenhouse – primarily, though not exclusively – from his highly acclaimed and influential book, *An Introduction to Curriculum Research and Development* (1975). A few short years later he wrote a draft paper *What counts as research?* that is available online.[1] In this work, Stenhouse (1980: 14) concludes that 'two points seem to me clear: first, teachers must inevitably be intimately involved in the research process; and second, researchers must justify themselves to practitioners, not practitioners to researchers'. In this and a previous work (Stenhouse, 1978) he draws upon history, theology, physics, philosophy, lexicography, and even biology, painting, social science, music and novels: a learned man! Eloquently, yet bluntly, he points out that teachers are in charge of classrooms and that they, not academic researchers, are better placed to carry out research.

Stenhouse argues persuasively that the prime function of education research is to assist teachers with their professional judgements – and this is how I chanced upon Bawtry Mayflower primary school.

Pilgrims' progress

Early in 2015, I attended a meeting of university staff with a few head teachers, none of whom I had met before; and I raised the issue of practitioner enquiry. Somewhat brazenly, I distributed copies of a journal by then College of Teachers,[2] titled *Education Today* – it was a special issue themed on practitioner enquiry (Luby, 2014). I invited conversation. The three head teachers – Kevin Flint, Julie Jenkinson and Janet Witton – all responded positively.[3] This led to an invitation from Julie to work with Bawtry Mayflower primary school staff.

Prior to meetings with staff, Julie briefed me of the appraisal system whereby teaching staff had four personal targets each year – one of which had to be an evidence-based topic. That is to say, each teacher had to select a topic for investigation and report upon their progress at a subsequent staff meeting. We agreed that I would have a consultancy role with the staff whereby I would listen to their plans, progress, difficulties concerning their chosen topics and offer some advice.

Joy. It is a joy to be in the company of dedicated staff as they talk about their hopes, plans, ambitions for their pupils. How they are teaching. What they are teaching. What they are learning. How their pupils respond. Anecdotes. Evidences – in its broadest sense. The staff seek clues from myriad sources. Pupils' smiles. Off-the-cuff comments. The 'feel' of their classrooms. But they also value, highly, evidence that is objective. Tests. Attainment targets. Progress rates. After all, this is how they are judged by the outside world.

Around half of the staff select an evidence target from the School Improvement Plan – the other half choose a topic that interests them. During the 45 minutes' conversations with pairs of staff, I come to appreciate that this is a school 'in which teachers are encouraged and trusted to collaborate, investigate, experiment and take informed risks' (Walker et al., 2019). This is a school in which I would like to have taught. And this high regard is confirmed later by a delegation of Netherlands' school leaders as they tour Bawtry Mayflower school. I see the school through their eyes – I hear their comments – and they, too, are impressed.

During our consultancies, advice is offered to staff about how they are conducting their evidence-based investigations. Further support by email is also offered and is accepted by some. Returning the following year, I ascertain that advice has been rejected, ignored, accepted, modified. Just how it should be. The teachers are the experts. Their school. Their children. Their curricula.

Two teachers stand out from a research perspective: Julia Crawshaw and Claire Dunn. They exemplify the finding of the BERA (2014: 20) report that 'for those teachers who have engaged successfully with and in research, there is little doubt that the curriculum and pedagogic innovation and change that have followed has been very powerful'.[4]

To begin with, neither Julia nor Claire were interested in research. Like the large majority of teachers undertaking research for the first time – it is seen as an imposition. Indeed, there is often an undercurrent of resentment. However, in the case of both Claire and Julia once they witnessed the positive effects that their research topics were having on their pupils' learning – then, in their own words, they became 'hooked'. Now, they are advocates for an evidence-based approach to teaching.

Their work has been peer reviewed and can be found online: Crawshaw (2017) and Dunn (2017). Quality is to be found in the presentation – with thanks to California-based Social Publishers Foundation. Quality is also found in the impacts upon the school – role play to improve boys' writing and parental engagement with homework. Recommendations made and conclusions drawn are sound. Sure, the evidence is limited, imperfect: but isn't all research? Good research findings draw attention to their limitations. Neither Claire nor Julia seek perfection – they seek to make wise, professional judgements in order to enhance the learning experiences of their children. And, as Stenhouse would have it, their evidence-based projects have enhanced the quality of their decision making and their children's learning.

The conversation

Around the time of the autumn 2017 visit by the school leaders and teachers from the Netherlands, I was aware that there had been some further progress with research regarding Bawtry Mayflower primary school. Doncaster Research School had come into existence. Julie Jenkinson, the head teacher had been contacted and was involved in some capacity. Some 18 months later I had the pleasure of meeting up with both Julie and Claire in their school for a professional conversation.

Wednesday, 1 May 2019
Bawtry, South Yorkshire

AL: And we had the conference and all that so you were just beginning to tell me; but what's happened since?

JULIE JENKINSON: Lots and lots and lots!

AL: Can you update me then please?

JULIE: I became involved with the research school and that was two years ago, just over two years ago? … It's Doncaster Research School, through Partners in Learning, so Partners in Learning is a teaching school in Doncaster …

So, it's EEF [Education Endowment Foundation] basically and it just seemed to fit where we needed to be … I took up this role with the research school; its primary strategic lead and it's just that I've got my eye on primaries … And really, just like … the learning from that has just been exponential. It's been brilliant. So I got to go on some conferences … met people from all the other research schools up and down the country.

… So, yeah, the training has been phenomenal and so you're hearing from people who are really in the know; and then had access to good training and people who just are really up to date with everything.

AL: Could you give me an example of what you call good training? …

JULIE: Yes, so … well for example, we went to Blackpool to the Research Conference there and that was training but … part of that was around CPD [continued professional development] for staff and making sure that staff have got that understanding of … there's a theoretical basis for CPD which we always try to do I think but I think we're much better at …

Notably, a survey by Nelson et al. (2017) questioned teachers about the relative influence that different sources of information had on their decisions about pedagogy or whole-school change. In this report they discovered that information based on academic research had only a small to moderate influence on teachers' decision making; and the findings from Walker et al. (2019) were very similar. Perhaps, though, Julie's comments about a theoretical base for CPD suggest that research schools are beginning to have an impact and that academic-based research may become a more important influence:

AL: But how has it impacted upon practice? What are you actually doing differently here in Bawtry Mayflower that you didn't do before?

JULIE: Right, so the action research – we've just moved away from that model and what we do now is we're just calling it Practitioner Enquiry and its more focused; so, rather than teachers having free reign –

CLAIRE DUNN: Bawtry Mayflower's Disciplined Inquiry Approach and it's based on the EEF's 5 Steps School Improvement Cycle; so, it's got five steps and it really mirrors the School Improvement Cycle that's recommended by the EEF. (See Figure 4.1.)

Bawtry Mayflower primary school has taken on board the EEF's 5 Steps School Improvement Plan (SIP) and has put it into practice. This is in conjunction with the Disciplined Inquiry Approach. Like appreciative inquiry, discussed previously, the Disciplined Inquiry Approach is not widely known within the world of UK education. However, it has a rich history. Lee Shulman, professor emeritus at Stanford Graduate School of Education, and renowned for his concept of pedagogical content knowledge (PCK) discusses disciplines of inquiry in education in an early 1980s paper for the American Educational Research Association (Shulman, 1981). Within a UK context it has been brought into vogue by Dylan Wiliam, at a 2014 researchED conference, and spread by 'leading lights' such as Gary Jones[5] and Alex Quigley.[6]

Step 1: *Decide what you want to achieve.*
Identify school priorities using data and your professional judgement e.g.
- Families of Schools Databases i.e. find out how your school compares to other, similar schools (database has 15,000+ primary schools and 3,000+ secondary schools).
- Assessing and Monitoring Pupil Progress. A 16-page guide to help track pupils' progress and assess their mastery of knowledge and concepts.

Step 2: *Identify possible solutions.*
- Consider a range of high-quality evidence to inform your choices.
- Teaching and Learning Toolkit. An accessible summary of the international evidence on teaching 5–16 year olds.
- Early Years Toolkit. An accessible summary of educational research for Early Years teaching.
- Promising Projects. EEF-funded projects which have shown promising results when trialled.

Step 3: *Giving it the best chance of success.*
Identify and apply the ingredients of effective implementation.
- Putting Evidence to Work – A School's Guide to Implementation (Early Years, Primary and Secondary). A 44-page guidance report.

Step 4: *Evaluating impact.*
Determine the impact of change and identify potential improvements for the future.
- DIY Evaluation Guide. An interactive tool supporting teachers to conduct evaluations of new programmes in your own contexts.

Step 5: *Securing and spreading change.*
Mobilise the knowledge and use the findings to inform the work of the school to grow or stop the intervention.
- Research Schools Network.
- Strategic School Improvement Fund.

Figure 4.1 EEF 5 Steps School Improvement Plan
Source: https://educationendowmentfoundation.org.uk/tools/5-steps-to-applying-evidence-in-your-school/

In terms of specifics for Bawtry Mayflower primary school then …

AL: Was it something in the School Development Plan or you just followed things you're interested in? …

CLAIRE: Well this time … these ones are based on, yeah, School Improvement Priorities; so this year it's spelling. So, all teachers are working in phases and they were given … I pointed them to different kinds of evidence banks that they could use, so they've all researched spelling and different strategies for spelling. They created an enquiry plan and we use like the EEF's tool for planning and enquiry, so they've looked at outcomes. They've looked at all the data, they've looked at the active ingredients of the approach and things. So we're in a stage now where the … everybody did baselines of data as a starting point and now the … enquiries are kind of in process really in the classrooms with the children.

[…]

JULIE: My perception is that the staff are fantastic … all of them and because they are so involved in the whole process of those children's learning and wanting it to be the best and because there's lots of discussion. Although, yeah, they all knew that spelling was an issue and we'd all discussed it, what is it, we've tried this, we've tried this, we've tried this and ultimately it wasn't the system; it wasn't whether we used 'no nonsense' spelling or 'Read Write Inc.' spelling. It was about the *rigour* [emphasis added] that it was done and are we actually doing the right thing? The why of it. So unpicking that and then being part of it; they're just fine with it and the working in groups is really supportive.

AL: I was kind of angling towards that because I thought that might be a selling point that you'd actually collaborated in working together?

JULIE: Yeah. Yeah. Yeah.

AL: And now you have a common focus, you're focusing on spelling, you can share that.

JULIE: Yes.

AL: Whereas, if you've got individual different projects, well that might be of interest to you but not of interest to anybody else in the school.

CLAIRE: Yeah, and I think they can see the bigger picture so the last step is about it building into and like spreading and securing the change, so it's all about the interventions that people have tried. So after they've been evaluated thinking about what's been successful, what's worthy of kind of sharing across school and then that will inform the action plan for spelling.

In my early contacts with Bawtry Mayflower primary school, I was impressed with the teachers' involvement with practitioner enquiry and that it was clearly encouraged and supported by the head teacher. But they have moved on. Previously, the practitioner enquiries were interesting and of value – but to a limited audience. The practitioner enquiries into role play and homework by Julia and Claire had intrinsic value to them and they were of potential interest to fellow teachers in the early years. Furthermore, they promulgated their work through publication online (Crawshaw, 2017; Dunn, 2017) and conference presentation.[7] All of this is admirable. However, through adoption of the EEF's 5 Steps SIP in combination with a Disciplined Inquiry Approach – the school now has a more disciplined, systematic and rigorous approach to evidence-based practice.

Rigour, discipline and a systematic approach to educational research are of interest at the highest levels of intellectual pursuit (Bridges, 2019; Keiner, 2019) and they are considered by Dimmock (2013) in a homage to Lawrence Stenhouse:[8]

> writing in the 1970s ... his pioneering work bringing research and practice together was decades ahead of its time ... We should continually remind ourselves of our indebtedness to him ... [and] build on the foundations he left ... How could practitioner research fulfil (his) requirements of being systematic, planned, rigorous and self-critical?

The conversational comments of both Julie and Claire above suggest that Stenhouse's foundations are being built upon. Bawtry Mayflower's combination of EEF's 5 Steps and a Disciplined Inquiry Approach satisfy his requirements of practitioner research being 'systematic, planned, rigorous and self-critical'.

Another notable feature is that through a more systematic, evidence-based approach to school improvement the teaching staff at Bawtry Mayflower now take a longer-term view of educational change:

JULIE: ... because the one thing that we've got really good at is understanding none of this is a quick fix, we've got to just bide our time. So our School Improvement Plan, we've changed that completely how we work now and it's ... we used to do a School Improvement Plan year on year and sometimes things rolled over. But it was more ... incidental I think. Now our plan is based on three years and each year ... so we have things ... well I'll show you. (See Table 4.1.)

AL: So being so heavily involved with research has now kind of encouraged you to think much longer term?

JULIE: Yeah and it's around the ... you know the Schools Guide to Implementation, so the EEF ...

CLAIRE: That one.

JULIE: Document. So it's around the different phases of implementing something successfully and it's going for that sustained change. You can't make a change without going through the stages but that actually those stages that could be three years. So you could spend a whole year just exploring the issue and exploring different solutions.

CLAIRE: Which is where we are with our spelling.

JULIE: Yeah.

CLAIRE: We've been doing that all year.

AL: And so ... are you quite comfortable with that then?

JULIE: Hmm!

AL: Because you see that's what other people, whereas in the past you might have got a bit ... oh they should really be further on; they should be doing more or ...?

JULIE: I think it's ... because of all the reading we've done and because of an understanding of this model. Yeah, I suppose it gives you the confidence but it does sort of make sense. But maybe whereas ... so for example, if Ofsted came along and our spelling outcomes were not as good as they should be and they were questioning the way we teach spelling, I would feel quite comfortable in sort of arguing our case for the reasons we're doing it. Yeah, there is an issue, we know there's an issue.

Table 4.1 Extract from Bawtry Mayflower SIP 2018-2021

Improvement Priority	Action / Intervention	Timescale	Budget / Resource Implications	Monitoring	Success Criteria
Strengthen the culture of research across the school	New Research Lead role developed through work with research school [RS]. RS lead to support all staff with involvement in Disciplined Inquiry (DI) – Whole school focus on vocabulary and spelling	Summer 2019	Time for CD and JULIE to attend RS training as required – note: school receives payment for RS work. Professional development [PD] for all staff. Time for staff to work together. JULIE and CD continue to work together with RS. Impact – PD in school / learning from and with others. Whole school DI for Spelling in place	JULIE / RS	All staff to be confident in using research evidence to support teaching and learning
	Support Education Endowment Foundation trials: Easy Peasy and Rosendale Metacognition trial. Action plan for improvement – plan to include Intent, Implementation, Impact of role	September 2019			

AL: So we're addressing it.

JULIE: But before, when we've jumped in and tried to buy a new scheme; it's not worked. So we're looking for that long-term goal and it's the same with the reading.

CLAIRE: Yes. Yeah.

JULIE: So the reading –

CLAIRE: So we've completely changed the way that we teach reading; but again it's not a quick fix and it's so complex. But it's all rooted in evidence and research; but it's taking a long time to see the results. It's not something that we could put in place and then a year later we could see the impact in SATs [Standard Assessment Tests] results.

JULIE: It's that cycle all the time of just keep revisiting what we've done, evaluating it, making any changes again; and it's that cycle of improvement.

Given the recent history of collaboration and practitioner enquiry within Bawtry Mayflower primary school there are good grounds for believing that a systematic, evidence-based approach to educational practices will prosper here. Indeed, in some respects, Bawtry is a role model for other schools under the umbrella of the Doncaster Research School. However, Bawtry itself can rightfully be described as a leafy, market town and is atypical of towns and villages in the Metropolitan Borough of Doncaster. There has to be a 'question mark' as to whether practices in Bawtry Mayflower school will transfer readily across to schools in less affluent and more challenging socio-economic circumstances.

Helpfully, such a comparator school is to be found just under 10 miles away in a south-westerly direction. Crossing over the old Great North Road (A1) and into the bordering county of Nottinghamshire, one arrives at Carlton-in-Lindrick – and Ramsden primary school.

Notes

1 This is a draft paper from which Lawrence Stenhouse asks 'not to be quoted'. Given that both he and the University of East Anglia's Centre for Applied Research in Education are no longer with us; and, above all, given the quality of Stenhouse's work, I have set aside this request.

2 A predecessor organisation from which the Chartered College of Teaching inherited its royal charter.

3 Kevin and Janet were head teachers of Dunsville primary school and Lakeside primary school respectively – both Doncaster schools.

4 This quote taken from background paper 7 that was commissioned for this BERA report: Leat, D., Lofthouse, R. and Reid, A. *Teachers' views: perspectives on research engagement.*

5 e.g. see Evidence Based Educational Leadership blog, 14 June 2015, at http://evidencebasededucatio nalleadership.blogspot.com/2015/06/disciplined-inquiry.html

6 e.g. see Developing 'Disciplined Inquiry' blog, 30 June 2017, at https://researchschool.org.uk/hun-tington/blog/developing-disciplined-inquiry

7 Evidence-based Approaches to Closing the Gap, regional conference, Bishop Grosseteste University, Lincoln, June 2016.

8 Professor Dimmock is based at the Robert Owen Centre for Educational Change, University of Glasgow, that 'aims to promote more equitable education systems through theory-driven applied research underpinned by a commitment to the principles of social justice and lifelong learning' (University website www.gla.ac.uk).

References

BERA (British Educational Research Association). 2014. [Online] *Research and the teaching profession: building the capacity for a self-improving education system.* Available from: www.thersa.org/globalassets/pdfs/bera-rsa-research-teaching-profession-full-report-for-web-2.pdf [Accessed 27 August 2019]

Bridges, D. 2019. [Online] 'Rigour', 'discipline' and the 'systematic' in educational research – and why they matter. *European Education Research Journal*. 21 August 2019. Available from: https://journals.sagepub.com/doi/abs/10.1177/1474904119868558?journalCode=eera [Accessed 28 August 2019]

Crawshaw, J. 2017. [Online] *Engaging boys in writing through role play: following their lead.* Available from: www.socialpublishersfoundation.org/knowledge-base/engaging-boys-in-writing-through-role-play-following-their-lead/ [Accessed 27 August 2019]

Dimmock, C. 2013. [Online] *Knowledge is the route to emancipation: Lawrence Stenhouse on teacher work.* Available from: http://robertowencentre.academicblogs.co.uk/knowledge-is-the-route-to-emancipation-lawrence-stenhouse-on-teacher-work/ [Accessed 28 August 2019]

Dunn, C. 2017. [Online] *Engaging children and parents in homework.* Available from: www.socialpublishersfoundation.org/knowledge-base/engaging-children-and-parents-in-homework/ [Accessed 27 August 2019]

Keiner, E. 2019. [Online] 'Rigour', 'discipline' and the 'systematic': the cultural construction of educational research identities? *European Education Research Journal*. 24 January 2019. Available from: https://journals.sagepub.com/doi/10.1177/1474904118824935?icid=int.sj-abstract.similar-articles.1 [Accessed 28 August 2019]

Luby, A. 2014. Editorial. *Education Today: Journal of the College of Teachers*. Special issue themed on practitioner enquiry, Winter 64(4) 1-2.

Nelson, J., Mehta, P., Sharples, J. and Davey, C. 2017. [Online] *Measuring teachers' research engagement: findings from a pilot study*. March 2017. London: Education Endowment Foundation. Available from: https://educationendowmentfoundation.org.uk/public/files/Evaluation/Research_Use/NFER_Research_Use_pilot_report_-_March_2017_for_publication.pdf [Accessed 27 August 2019]

Shulman, L. S. 1981. Disciplines of inquiry in education: an overview. *Educational Researcher* 10(6) 5-12+23.

Stenhouse, L. 1975. *An Introduction to Curriculum Research and Development*. London: Heinemann.

Stenhouse, L. 1978. [Online] *Applying research to education*. Draft paper. Centre for Applied Research in Education, University of East Anglia. September 1978. Available from: www.uea.ac.uk/documents/4059364/4994243/Stenhouse-1978-Applying+Research+to+education.pdf/24ec7b40-ac56-46d2-8f8f-2bb7b4c53ac4 [Accessed 27 August 2019]

Stenhouse, L. 1980. [Online] *What counts as research?* Draft paper. Centre for Applied Research in Education, University of East Anglia. December 1980. Available from: www.uea.ac.uk/documents/4059364/4994243/Stenhouse-1980-What+counts+as+research.pdf/416a405d-4e84-46a0-b4d9-cbd31815ade7 [Accessed 27 August 2019]

Walker, M., Nelson, J. and Bradshaw, S. with Brown, C. 2019. [Online] *Teachers' engagement with research: what do we know? A research briefing*. May 2019. London: Education Endowment Foundation/National Foundation for Educational Research. Available from: https://educationendowmentfoundation.org.uk/public/files/Evaluation/Teachers_engagement_with_research_Research_Brief_JK.pdf [Accessed 27 August 2019]

5 *Audaces fortuna juvat*
Fortune favours the bold

Audaces fortuna juvat – Fortune favours the bold. So runs the motto of Ramsden primary school: and the school lives up to its motto. However, I was oblivious to this when driving to Carlton-in-Lindrick for my first full meeting with head teacher Chris Wilson. Driving out of Blyth, the winding road and the lush countryside of Hodsock Priory caught my attention. Entering via the southern route from Worksop, a mere 3 miles away, first impressions are of a pretty village. This is unlike the other schools in the Ad Astra Primary Partnership. This is no Bowbridge housing scheme. Nor former mining stock like Jacksdale, Kirkby in Ashfield and New Ollerton. Rather, it is more akin to Bawtry – or so I thought – but appearances can deceive.

Winter 2016

My earlier, brief meetings with the head teacher, Chris Wilson, had gone well:

> An integral feature of Ad Astra life is the half-termly meetings that are preceded by socialising over lunch; and this socialising is crucial to the success of these meetings. Indeed, it was through this pre-lunch socialising that I was introduced to Ad Astra. To begin with, I felt a little like a 'fish out of water'. A secondary school practitioner – from another country, Scotland: what did I have in common with these East Midlands head teachers? The answer? Passion. Passion for football, passion for learning, passion for theology and, of course, passion for teaching.
>
> Discussion about the merits, demerits and seemingly endless demise of three great football clubs – Celtic, Nottingham Forest and Sunderland – revealed something of our hinterlands – we had shared common interests outside the school. Passion for learning demonstrated that we had insights to offer each other about school, pedagogy, class-room life. Passion for theology opened the way to an unexpected hour-long encounter about Catholicism, Judaism and the mysteries of life. And yes, passion for teaching – the passion that mesmerises John Hattie in *Visible Learning* and the bond that unites us all.
>
> (Luby 2019: 35)

Chris is the Sunderland fan with whom I was about to share an unexpected and engaging theological discussion. At this visit I met too with his staff: unfailingly welcoming. Cheek-by-jowl with a teacher colleague in a juniors' classroom, I was reminded how easy it can be to forge a bond with a fellow teacher. She shared her current classroom experiences and I shared my past ones. There were similarities – and differences: but mostly similarities. Schools are schools. Classes are classes. Children are children.

Taking a tea break in the staffroom: a wave of nostalgia. Less than two years out of the classroom – seated softly – peacefulness, 'at home'. The incomplete timetable pinned on the wall; the strewn messiness of papers and documents and, of course, the inevitable biscuits. But Ramsden was a 'gently, gently' affair. My visit was taking place immediately after a two-day visitation from the inspectors (2–3 February 2016) – and their subsequent rating of 'Good' (Ofsted, 2016). And this visit proves useful – more than. A gently, gently approach is well received: teachers relax, open up. The notion of 'professional conversation' starts to firm up (Luby, 2016).

Spring 2019

Leaving behind the cathedral city of Lincoln in the autumn of 2017 entailed a farewell to the Ad Astra partnership and there had been no further contact with Chris – other than a wee message to arrange this meeting. What awaits?

Monday, 29 April 2019
Carlton-in-Lindrick, near Worksop

AL: We're at Ramsden primary school with Chris Wilson who's the head teacher and Chris, I was just recalling the first time that I came here. This school, this area is very pretty, it's very picturesque but you soon disabused me of that notion. Could you maybe expand upon that please? [...]

CHRIS: Yeah, in the 1970s there was a load of high-rise flats that were knocked down in Worksop town centre and a big estate was built just across the fields here. And this school that has been here for 200 years traditionally was meant for the people, I suppose, that worked for the squire; and who now have these very expensive stone houses that are a throwback to the squire's days, if you like. And this school was the catchment area for those, I suppose; and all the rough kids, as it were, went to the newly built school that was purpose built for all the families that were moved from the high rise flats and into the estate just behind our fields; and they went there. But I suppose as the years have gone on that kind of ... some of ... well I don't know, how many children around here went to Kingston – but quite a lot of the children from the estate came to ours – to the extent where it's now nearly 90% of the children that come to Ramsden primary school are from the estate, that is, shall we say, fondly referred to as 'The Bronx'.

This struck a chord. In a previous life I took up beat duties in Livingston, West Lothian. A new town, pleasing to the eye; but displeasing crime figures. Noting my Glasgow accent the shift sergeant assigned me to Knightsridge on the basis that we all 'spoke the same language'. As Glasgow residents were decanted to Livingston; so too Worksop residents to Carlton-in-Lindrick. Sadly, as Glasgow folk spiked the crime rates in Livingston; so too, Worksop folk to Carlton-in-Lindrick.[1]

Challenging circumstances call for bold measures and the school motto for Ramsden primary suggests that the head teacher and the school staff are bold. I reckon, though, it is better if you decide for yourself ...

AL: Okay so ... now Ad Astra ... What's your thoughts on it looking back?

CHRIS: I thought it was ... a great idea at the time. I thought it was inspiring by Wendy to get some of the schools that she thought were addressing the kind of poverty issues that ... affect their educational lives; and the fact that we were all in a wide-ranging area so that there was no kind of direct competition – which meant that we were confident enough to work with each other and share ideas. I don't know if the original idea was to get us all to become a kind of academy system ourselves ... it didn't come out like that in the end. But I think the stuff that was kicked off by it was certainly very interesting and it's something that I went on to study for my Masters and now want to carry on with, with my PhD. And the Perspectives of Poverty which Wendy came up with I think are ... they were good then and they're still relevant, very relevant now. So ...

AL: So, is there any of those five perspectives ... my recollection is that each school was supposed to kind of focus on one of the perspectives, kind of specialise in that and then move onto another.

CHRIS: Yeah.

AL: So which one did you ... which one did Ramsden focus on?

CHRIS: We were working on the poverty of experience and ambition and hopefully working on future jobs, future careers which we actually went on to do something with Together for Worksop and ... we ended up working with the sixth form college in Retford and ... all the Year 6 children in all the primary schools around Worksop were invited to go to the ... Post 16 Centre in Retford where they were having this kind of market place where they could learn about the future careers and jobs. Because a lot of times what we found was that by the time children were making their choices about what they wanted to be, they were making choices that weren't compatible with their ultimate ambition. So, we realised, 'Well, children need to try and have a think about what they want to be a little bit earlier ...' but also for the parents, so that they could have some sort of viewpoint and road map about how they were actually going to get from A to B if you like.

AL: ... So, you are kind of saying by late primary they should actually be thinking of spreading, expanding their horizon and thinking wider and greater?

CHRIS: Well, yes, to a certain extent; but also then containing it as well ... because ... we've found that it's only when kids start hitting Year 3 and 4 that they start then wanting to become U-Tubers. It's not even footballers anymore ... now it's U-Tubers, it's somewhere else that gets money very, very quickly. So your kind of ambition to be a lawyer or your ambition to be this, that's still not around. Its 'I want to be rich and if I can't do it by being a footballer, I'll do it by showing people how to put makeup on through U-Tube videos ...' So it was that kind of thing that we tried to show well fine, just like when I wanted to be a footballer, 'don't give up your dream' – but realise that it might not happen and you need to think about what else you might be able to do as well.

AL: So, what exactly do you do in the school then to encourage them to think about their ambitions?

CHRIS: ... first of all we started just having a look at the kind of opportunities and jobs that our parents were doing and asking parents if they would come in. A lot were basically electricians, nurses ... one of our parents who's a nurse just said to us that she had a friend who was a doctor that worked at the hospital and he could come in as well; and we were over the moon at the idea of getting in a doctor as well.

[...]

Pierre Bourdieu and the idea of the doctor and the habitus and all of this kind of thing ... it's about understanding and if the children are just trained to pass the exams in numeracy or English, whether it's reading or writing. Yeah, they will be able to do that; but if they haven't got the additional wider knowledge then they're still going to end up down that narrow path and not realise about what kind of opportunities are open for them.

AL: And does it not now give them more reason to want to do the drill and the learning because they can now see an ambition that could be realised?

CHRIS: Absolutely –

AL: There's a purpose to this numeracy, this writing, it will enable you at some point in the future to become a nurse, a doctor, an electrician?

CHRIS: Exactly! The children at the moment are just in danger constantly of being ... misunderstanding the fact that ... they're just being drilled, or they're just being taught; and if they don't understand why they're being taught it, then they're not going to find it as attractive as if they've realised that, well, in actual fact ... I'd love to do this for a job, or ... what do we need to do to be able to do that? Well, you need this, or you need that, or you need an understanding of science, or you need an understanding of maths; then they'll actually think that there is more of a purpose in doing it.

[...]

AL: ... What is it you really want them to achieve?

CHRIS: What we want to achieve is to get the ambition of understanding what they can achieve... and if we can get the parents to understand right from a very early age that these kinds of things are possible, then that's what we'll try and do. So I've been talking about university; but what we're trying to do then is take it all the way back down then to an 18 month old child; and then think about how we can affect the parents of that 18 month old child –

AL: How do you?

[...]

CHRIS: Well, first of all, it basically started from ... the Together for Worksop meetings we found that health was just ... having more and more cutbacks. So we thought, 'Well, the only way that we could do that is if we employ these kinds of people ourselves.' I came across a school nurse who was retiring, got fed up with the admin and all that kind of thing; and she said, 'Do you know, if I could just have a job for two or three days a week I'd be over the moon.' So, I said, 'Well, funnily enough, this is what we would like to do' – and where we started to develop ... we could have a parents course and all these parents courses could have a focus every week. So we decided that it would be very early language: how do you develop language in 18 month old children? How do you develop healthy sleeping patterns; how do you develop healthy eating patterns; because we thought if we could develop all of these kinds of healthy choices in the parents while the children were 18 months old then that could be the very start, if you like, of how we could affect children coming to our primary school. Not just at the age of 5 when we get them; but actually at the age of 18 months which is well before we get them. But if we could get parents to come in at that age we're already 2½ years ahead of ourselves.

AL: So, to me, you're really broadening the understanding of education because you're now saying we're not just here to educate the children, we're actually here to educate the parents?

CHRIS: The parents as well, yeah, which is why our new hash tag is 'your kids are our kids' because basically this is our viewpoint of it ...[2]

[...]

I think again there were certain things that used to annoy me from the health perspective. There were quite a few kids that needed a lot of speech and language therapy [SALT] and ... classes, if you like, were always put in the community centre, or the health centre, or ... wherever it was; but not school and the parents wouldn't take their kids. Or they would miss appointments, and ... once you've missed three appointments they just knocked it on the head and you would have to go through the whole process of re-referring them ... And one day, I said, 'Look, why don't you [take] speech and language classes in school, the children are already here, you come and teach the kids in school?' 'Oh no, no, we can't do that.' I thought, it was just one of things, why not? So I decided, well, if you're not going to do that I'll buy somebody in; and we just bought from the health service speech and language therapists, experts and things like that to actually come in.

AL: That's what Jo Cook did at Hallcroft, she did that. She did almost like a little experiment and that was professional development – because that was to deliberately help the teachers to increase their understanding. So SALT came in and did so much work; but with a view to the teachers are going to take this on – because we kind of trained you up over a period of time. I mean, some people might say this is a bad thing that you're taking on functions which the council should be doing. You're taking on all these extra functions which are disappearing from the council so that could be seen as a negative ...

To me the way you're talking ... the classroom boundary walls have just disappeared. They're all melted, they've gone [emphasis added].

[...]

AL: So, I'm thinking of leadership; so you've got all these things that you're talking about just now, how do you lead the staff forward with these? ... How do you know they buy into it?

CHRIS: Because of the amount of things that they actually come up and bring ideas now. I mean, for example, we've got the sign specialist, Mrs Campbell, who we were invited to ... we went down to the House of Lords just a few months ago because we were the only primary school in the country to be nominated for the Outstanding Science Technology Engineering Mathematics [STEM] Club Award. So, we went down to the House of Lords. Today we've just booked another train ticket because, yet again, we've been put through to the regional final of another STEM Club Award; and if we win that, we'll go back down to London again to the Royal Society ... so Francesca is emailing me over the weekend saying 'I've just found this on Facebook', or 'I've just found this on somewhere'. Eleanor will email me at the weekend, 'I've just found this or I've just found that' because of all the different kinds of interests that we've got that are related to the Perspectives of Poverty.

[...]

CHRIS: When I very first came to the school, one member of staff mentioned a child who had not made any progress within a particular timeframe and said, 'Well, what do you expect, they come from that estate.' And we've moved from that to where we are now – where everything that we do, we try and give the kids the best kind of opportunities that we can get. So, you know, we're constantly thinking about how we can change something else. So, our homework policy is now what we call Branching Out. So, instead of us giving just something that's Maths, English related; our homework activity will last over half term – and we'll say, right go to the Science Museum or go to here, go to there and, basically, what we're trying to do is broaden their experiences. Rather than just sitting at the table doing an English task, or a maths task, or something like that ...

[...]

AL: Could you just give me an example, what's ... you can anonymise it or generalise it, give me an example of what you might discuss with a teacher and how you would know by the end of the year the success or otherwise?

CHRIS: Well, what I would like to try and do is ... for example, one of the teachers is a music specialist; so in her appraisal I would talk about her being the music specialist – but then think about how music could be brought into the curriculum ... she might think, 'Right, one of the easiest things is to teach times tables by doing it by song.' You know, you chant the times tables to a tune, you learn that. That would be an easy way of bringing that in. One of the more difficult things of bringing it in is like, 'Okay, so we're thinking about speech and language as being the thing about the Perspectives of Poverty, about the poverty of language. So how can we bring that music thing into speech and language?' So, voice coaching, you've seen these choir people that do the ... all the different weird kind of sounds that the voice can make ... So this person is a music specialist ... if we train all the children ... in voice techniques to do all of these different sounds on the voice, all the different muscles that develop speech and develop singing, will develop their speech and language ability ... have a look how your specialist subject can be converted into the five steps of poverty because there will always be a way – and then the members of staff have that kind of wide-ranging kind of free flow; because I think when people are given that kind of freedom of expression, they think of different ways of bringing it in.

[...]

AL: But you do need a framework; so you're telling me the five poverty criteria are still ... that's your template for the school?

CHRIS: That's now become not just ... as it was in the Ad Astra, the new Ofsted framework if you like is to ... getting schools to think about how their curriculum is unique to them and we moved ... to keep the learning outside the classroom and the STEM stuff and every- thing else that ... those ... five Perspectives of Poverty are now our whole kind of raison d'être if you like ...

AL: So is that in your School Development Plan?

CHRIS: Yeah. Yeah. That's in the School Development Plan and we have the A3 whiteboards which have all of the Perspectives of Poverty in the staffroom; and that is for every member of staff to freely have the whiteboard marker, I've got an idea that fits this perspective, or that perspective; and we write on it and we discuss it and see how we can bring it into every aspect of our curriculum.

AL: So how does that bit work then, so if you walked into the staffroom and you thought 'Oh! that's two new ideas', how do you then formalise it, how do you then share it with –

CHRIS: Well, then, we would have the staff meeting on a Wednesday … we discuss the new things that have been written on the board; and it might just at that point be a kernel of an idea. But then you get the other people that have a science kind of slant on it, or a music kind of slant on it, or a mathematical slant on it and it just develops from that kernel of an idea.[3]

AL: So how often does that happen, would you say you discuss ideas from your whiteboard in the staffroom?

CHRIS: I would say that … I mean there are basic kinds of ideas that go on all the time, kind of thing; but probably twice every half term we'd come up with a new way of doing something. Or somebody might see something in the press, or on Facebook, or Pinterest and that will develop an idea into how we could do something else.

AL: So somebody might come in and say, 'Yes, I like all the things you're talking about and the things you do in the school; but how do you measure success? How can you show me in bold figures all these things you talk about are actually successful?'

CHRIS: Yeah. One of the things that we can do; I mean we're always looking for different ways of measuring success … we don't want anything that's measured in six months, or a year, or something like that. We want something that's measured over a timeframe because you then get a feel of what the school, or what we're trying to –

AL: What do you mean over a timeframe Chris, you mean over a longer period?

CHRIS: Yeah, it might be three or four years and it might be; Ofsted might not be here from one four-year period or five-year period to the next; but all the things that we've done in that five-year period. If we've got a little bit of evidence from everything that we've done it gets the train moving, if you like, so that Ofsted can think 'Yeah, this school is actually doing what it says on the tin' if you know what I mean? It's not just; it's not just a flash in the pan or it's not just for show, this school really is living, walking the walk or whatever; for want of a better –

AL: Yeah, I get from what you said earlier … you seem to me to be taking the attitude that as long as we're doing these good things and children have enriched learning experiences, all the rest of it, reading et cetera will take care of itself. Let's not focus on that; let's not focus on the tracks of the railway, let's enjoy the journey, let's look out the window. Let's be the fireman, let's be the stoker.

CHRIS: Exactly! That's the point of view of the school, don't think about Ofsted. Ofsted will come and Ofsted will go; but I always say to the teachers 'You know, if we do what we do, Ofsted is irrelevant because they will come and they will see what we do; and they'll go away again.' You don't have to focus on Ofsted or even the SATs, you don't have to focus on anything like that. Just do what we're doing and they'll automatically–

AL: And do you think the new changes will help, curricular changes will help the school?

CHRIS: Again, it's something that I don't really pay a great deal of focus on; because if it's something that we're doing anyway we don't need that kind of external kind of 'Well, this is what you should have been doing anyway because this is what we're telling you …' It's

Ofsted that should have been doing this anyway; so we won't be changing what we do. They'll be changing what they look at and that will be, hopefully, better for the school.

There is much to analyse in what Chris has to say. He speaks of allowing his 'members of staff have that kind of wide-ranging kind of free flow; because I think when people are given that kind of freedom of expression, they think of different ways of bringing it in' and, similarly, I wished this for Chris too. I believe that it gives an insight to the kind of leader that he is. In the above conversational extract, he speaks freely about:

- the inspiration of the Ad Astra partnership and its continuing impact within the school regarding the five Perspectives of Poverty;
- promoting ambition within both pupils and parents – realistic ambition – such that they have a road map for their future lives;
- bringing outside expertise from the health service such as SALT and eyesight specialism within the very fabric of the school itself;[4]
- staff generating an explosion of ideas – some of them award-winning;
- a broad-based, experiential approach to homework;
- an innovative use of staff's subject knowledge specialisms prompted by the five Perspectives of Poverty;
- being 'ahead of the curve' with respect to developing curricula fitted to a school's particular context through the adoption of a *Leerkracht* approach to curriculum development; and
- inculcating a long-term understanding of evaluation and gathering evidence and encouraging a relaxed approach to Ofsted demands.

For the moment, though, I shall content myself by reviewing his thoughts on competition and collaboration – a major theme within the opening two chapters of this book. And here's what Chris has to say ...

CHRIS: I suppose it is a kind of negative thing, I suppose; but anything to do with Teaching School Alliances, academies or anything like that, then I will just slam doors, not interested. Not interested.

AL: ... You're just going out and doing all that research, your Masters; and you're talking about Pierre Bourdieu. You've opened your mind to the big wide world outside. Surely, academies and research schools and ... I'm thinking of people like James Siddle. I think you met James Siddle. He came to one of the Ad Astra meetings and James is Head of a small primary school near Alford in Lincolnshire. He's Director of the Kyra Research School in Lincoln. These are really good head teachers who just want to make their schools a better place for their children to learn more; and they're open-minded. You could just chat to them.

CHRIS: I'm perfectly happy to chat to them. But, you see, one of the things that we did was we ... again the Pupil Premium Conference, we did it again, some talks to them and one of the audience was ... a regional Ofsted HMI ... [who] came up and said 'Oh, that was fantastic, that was brilliant. All the research that you're doing and things like that, have you never thought about giving it to the Teaching School Alliances?' Why would I do that?

AL: Why would you not? Why would you not share it with your colleagues?

CHRIS: I'm perfectly happy to share it; but what I'm driving at is it seems as if … it seems as if schools that are not academies are not getting any of the credit that they deserve … all the things will be shone on academies or Teaching School Alliances as leading the way … and then some schools that are working together like Helen[5] and myself, that are doing all this kind of thing. If you're not in a Teaching School Alliance or if you're not in an academy, they're not wanting to know. Don't want to know. But –

[…]

AL: People will get to know … I get the impression you maybe think somehow they're going to take you over or they're – […] It would be [to] collaborate with colleagues.

CHRIS: If you go back to the old days before Outwood Grange came to Worksop it was two kind of separate entities. There was Portland and there was Valley. There was the Portland family which had about 6-7 schools in it … I think there are 18 primary schools in Worksop and then you had the Valley family which had a similar kind of amount; and then Outwood Grange came and took over both; and what happened is as … a family of primary schools we then conglomerated. So there was all 18 within the same family … rather than have 2 smaller famil[ies]. And then as the academy system developed more what happened was some people became stand-alone academies. Some people went with this academy or that academy and some people went with another academy. So there are about 3-4 … maybe 5 different Academy Trusts that are now in what was that 18 school … primary family. And when it was a primary family, if you like, there was a lot of collaboration … Now, because there are different Academy Trusts that are part of that family, if you like, there is a lot more mistrust and a lot less collaborative working in that Worksop family of primary schools than there used to be. So, I look at it and I actually see that the Academy Trust system has damaged the collaboration that –

AL: The Academy Trust system has damaged trust; that's what you're saying?

CHRIS: Yeah.

AL: Is that just competition?

CHRIS: I don't think … do you know it's not competition because I never minded competition. Competition was part of what we all expected anyway if you know what I mean? We all knew –

AL: Is it a drive for uniformity; you are part of our five-school Academy Trust and this is the way we do things?

CHRIS: I mean, listen, the way I look at it is, head teachers are not naturally [second-in-command] are they? … Head teachers are natural leaders; especially if you like the pressure that Ofsted have put you under the last decade or whatever. Nobody in their right mind will become a head teacher unless they're actually driven to become leaders … If you're a number one, you're dying to put in place all these different kinds of things that you might think of; all the different initiatives that you and your staff might want to come along with. The Hub, the nursery that we've got; the parental kind of adult learning things that we're trying to do now. I can put those in place, I don't need to ask anybody's permission for that. I don't need to ask Nottinghamshire's permission to do that …

[…]

AL: So, you are sharing what you're doing because you're being asked, people are noticing what you're doing.

CHRIS: Yeah, well, absolutely; I'll share it with Nottinghamshire Education Authority and things like that. But, if you like, it's a fear of power, is that the kind of ... thing? I feel driven to think about all the different things that I can do for Ramsden primary school. If Ramsden primary school is taken over by an Academy Trust then what will happen is any ideas that we have, not just me, but any ideas that we as a staff have will always have to be run past a bigger person; and that takes our drive away from us. So that's why I suppose I resist that as much as I possibly can. I'll share it with anybody like Nottinghamshire ...

AL: No, I can see where you're coming from; because I can see the Academy Trust might say to you 'That's very interesting, Chris, but I'm afraid we do things differently here.'

CHRIS: Yeah.

AL: ... and there's a drive for uniformity. It's hard to create diversity within ... they talk about a Self-Supporting School System; I like that idea.

CHRIS: I like that idea.

AL: I like that idea because that gives you this kind of autonomy you're talking about... You're not firmly locked in with each other. You do need that freedom.

CHRIS: And I think that's why the Ad Astra thing was so good; because it gave you that kind of working together to formulate those ideas – where it wasn't under an academy system, where one person was telling the other people what to do. It was the genuine sharing of the ideas and doing it in that safe kind of knowledge that anything that I share with you is not going to mean that some of the parents might choose your school, rather than mine; because they were so far ... distantly away from each other. You could share without any kind of competitive risk if you know what I mean? There's always ... competition is good, it keeps you on your toes, don't get me wrong, let's be honest about that, there is no problem with competition. But it's the level of, you know, 'swimming in shark-infested waters'.

Despite all of Chris's innovations there is a yearning back to the past of local authorities. He cites the example of two families of Worksop primary schools that had close collaborative ties. Perhaps this is a rose-tinted view though. One can argue that if such high levels of collaboration and exchange of good ideas were taking place then why the need for academies, Trusts and Teaching School Alliances? Apparently, the arrival of the Academy Trust system has brought sub-divisions and even mistrust between schools. Why give competitor schools your best ideas? This is sad to see: but understandable. A strength of the Ad Astra partnership lay in there being no geographical competitiveness between the schools. However, this proved to be Ad Astra's undoing as the schools were too far apart to maintain close ties. As more schools joined – there being around a dozen just prior to its demise – there was talk of geographical clusters: but this never came to fruition.

From the perspective of a head teacher of a stand-alone school it seems that there is too much competition within England's system of school education.

With his family background of many summer caravan holidays in the Netherlands allied to a support (second to Sunderland, of course) for PSV Eindhoven, I invited Chris to accompany me on a trip over the North Sea to Rotterdam to meet with three primary school head teachers. I had enjoyed a fascinating exchange visit there in the spring of 2017 and was keen to return. And so in late May 2019, we found ourselves aboard the permanently berthed cruise ship *SS Rotterdam*.

Notes

1   E.g. see www.worksopguardian.co.uk/news/heartbreak-after-thieves-target-a-worksop-primary-school-three-times-in-less-than-two-weeks-1-9543072
2   Interestingly, this is exactly the position under *Common Law* as teachers are held to be '*in loco parentis*'.
3   This is similar to the Dutch *Leerkracht* in the following chapter.
4   See www.designhhw.com/ramsden-woodland-nursery-hub
5   Helen Chambers, head teacher of Abbey Hill school as discussed previously.

References

Hattie, J. 2012. *Visible Learning for Teachers: Maximizing Impact on Learning*. Abingdon, Oxon: Routledge.
Luby, A. 2016. Stars and saints: professional conversations for enhancing classroom practices. *Education Today. Journal of The College of Teachers* 66(3) 2–6.
Luby, A. 2019. To the stars: Ad Astra addressing poverty. In P. Beckley (Ed.) *Supporting Vulnerable Children in the Early Years*. London: Jessica Kingsley Publishers.
Ofsted. 2016. *Ramsden primary school report*. Available from: https://files.api.ofsted.gov.uk/v1/file/2546075 [Accessed 29 August 2019]

6 *Op weg naar Emmaus*

On the way to Emmaus

that same day two of them were going to a village called Emmaus, about seven miles from Jerusalem, and talking with each other about all ... that had happened. While they were talking and discussing, Jesus himself came near and went with them, but their eyes were kept from recognizing him.

(Luke 24:13-16. *The Holy Bible, NRSV*)

Context

The Bible tells us that the disciples left behind the cross on their way to Emmaus and, although they were in the presence of Jesus, he was unrecognised. Similarly, at Rotterdam's Emmaus Catholic primary school, the symbolic presence of Jesus is unrecognised as neither crucifix nor cross are to be seen. However, as Christ ultimately reveals Himself to his disciples so, likewise, His love is made present through the Emmaus teachers. This observation was formed at a visit to Emmaus school in the cool, spring season of 2017; and it was confirmed by a return visit in the hot, early summer season of 2019.

Located in the port city of Rotterdam, Emmaus is nominally a Catholic primary school – but there are almost no Catholics on the school roll.[1] Emmaus has a huge influx of immigrants from different faiths and as a member of the Rotterdam Association for Catholic Education (RVKO)[2] it 'offers parents and students high-quality, contemporary primary education based on a constantly renewing Catholic tradition' (rvko.nl). In the case of Emmaus, the Catholic tradition has been renewed through the educational influences of Montessori as mediated through the adoption, in every classroom, of Hattie's (2012) *Visible Learning*. How did this arise? The head teacher, Anke Langmuur, has been a school Principal for 25 years and, after 10 years in a Montessori school, which she started with 7 pupils and grew to 600, Anke sought change – and found Emmaus in Rotterdam.

Tuesday, 28 May 2019
Emmaus primary school, Rotterdam

AL: You were sent here?

ANKE: I told almost five years the RVKO that I want to change. I want to change to another school but they don't have the follow up for me of the other school ... So when they had a follow up for me they said, 'Okay, we have a follow up.' Five years later I'm now ... I want to go to the centre of Rotterdam. I want to go to the children that I have here.

AL: So did you think ... were you bringing Montessori with you, were you thinking what I've learnt –

ANKE: Exactly! Yes, only I don't talk about it; but Montessori is ownership and Montessori work from motivation yes. I think Hattie is saying the same only in the way of Hattie but ...

AL: So, you didn't come in and say we're going to do Montessori –

ANKE: No, of course not; because they would say there's the door! No! No! [Laughter] That's not ... that's not ... the Principals here they were 40 years together, 2 men, and they work also from –

AL: Top-down.

ANKE: Yeah, top-down. When I came that was the culture.

AL: So what did you do at the beginning when you ... in your first like few months –

ANKE: I started talking with the people, in that moment there were 60 people around here, now we have 90 ... So start with talking with them, what they like, what they don't like; if they were the Principal what they would want to change, what they would want that stays. Everyone ... with everyone ... I had a talk, I listened.

AL: And what did you do in response to listening to what they said?

ANKE: What they said was ... what I ... heard was that they want more ownership ... You have to do it yourself but it's a way of organising it. And 2015 John Hattie with ... look through the education with the eyes of the children and help teachers to ... to help students to be their own teacher. It's the same as Montessori is saying, help me doing it myself. That's what Montessori is saying. I think, 'Yes, that's evidence-based.' So, I stay in the evidence based ...

This is a very interesting link that Anke makes between Montessori and the evidence base for John Hattie's (2012) *Visible Learning*. Hattie's work derives from more than 800 meta-analyses of 50,000 research articles that includes about 150,000 effect sizes and 240 million students. This is an astonishing amount of evidence. And yet, despite being a self-proclaimed 'measurement person', Hattie makes repeated references to 'passion' within the opening pages of his book. Hattie combines an empirical approach to furthering knowledge of education with an interpretative approach to teaching. There is a recognition that teachers have a practical function, whereby they consider *informed explanations* of educational practice as a basis for their deliberations about what ought to be done in a particular situation (Carr, 1986).

This is reminiscent of Maria Montessori whose passion for education led her to undertake scientific observations of pupils' learning activities in order to improve their educational experiences (https://amshq.org/About-Montessori/History-of-Montessori/Who-Was-Maria-Montessori). It also brings to mind The Sir Donald Bailey Academy, Abbey Hill school, Jacksdale school, Bawtry Mayflower school, Ramsden primary school and their head teachers – Lee Hessey, Helen Chambers, Peter Stonier, Julie Jenkinson and Chris Wilson. Each and every one has a passion for improving the education of the children in their care – and all seek evidence-informed explanations as to how to bring this about. But not only are solutions sought from elsewhere, they are sought from within:

ANKE: There's a tipping point and I think my tipping point is now reached and it takes time. If it had my tempo it was much quicker. [Laughter] So, I have to sit on my hands and have patience because you need to take everybody with you. And ... today there are also two teachers who want to speak with me, went to another school and have seen something and they want to know because they want to do an experiment and there's ... yeah there are ... different people and there here, they stay here because they have the room to experiment. And there are also people who think, 'Oh, that experiment, I just want that.' I try to say to everybody, 'That you can do ... to stay close to yourself but always think in the ... what's important for the children.'

ANDRE[3]: The interests of the children is the most important thing.

ANKE: And that's the ...

AL: So, you're happy to have teachers who are willing to innovate and experiment but you're also happy to have teachers who are more steady and cautious –

ANKE: I think you need them both.

    [...]

AL: ... But you need them, you need them, the ... they stem from the ...

ANDRE: The voice of the minority.

ANKE: Yes.

ANDRE: Is important. Okay, so how to change cultures?

ANKE: Yes! Yes! It is a culture change because people are used to it that 40 years long ...

ANDRE: But you've transformed the school from a very conservative inward community to progressive and innovative and –

AL: You've done it in a short space of time: 2013 that's not long.

ANKE: Yes, it's okay. So, now we say, 'We go further with what we are doing and we give room to each other; and we have room to go a little bit like this; and then we have to go like this for the children.'

AL: So, you're saying you have a period of experimentation, innovation and then you kind of slow down?

ANDRE: I wait for the results of the experiment before I go into that so I'm not ... being part of the experiment myself. I wait until the results of the experiment are there and then I'll –

With Anke there is much talk of innovation and experiments as she encourages her staff to do this – but at their own pace. As well as Montessori and Hattie this approach also draws upon the Dutch concept of *Leerkracht* or 'learning power' – to which Andre had introduced me the previous evening during our professional conversation aboard the *SS Rotterdam*:

ANDRE: So there is a Dutch concept, I don't know if you've heard it, it's the 'steering paradox', literally the *steering paradox*. We know that people work harder if they have ownership, if they ... it's, it's, their thing they're doing. So bottom-up works better than top-down. Now, you're a school leader and you know that bottom-up works better than top-down; your paradox ... what can I do from the top to create bottom-up movement? Which always means that you have to respect autonomy, give people space, but what if they don't use the space or don't use it wisely? So ... what Anke did in her research ... they develop ... they design an intervention and they measure what it does. And what she did was she handpicked a number of colleagues/staff who got complete freedom, carte blanche, could do whatever ... dream your own education, your perfect education and I'll support you.

[...]

... it's about *empowerment* [Andre's emphasis]. If you want your staff to be the best teacher that they have in them, you have to appreciate their views and their professionalism. You have to give them autonomy, give them space, respect the choices that they make even if maybe they're not your ... what you would have chosen.

[...]

The dilemma is that autonomy and isolation are very closely related. Isolation is always a bad thing. Autonomy is good, isolation is bad; so the question is how do you prevent teachers from thinking they are using their autonomy while, in fact, they closed the door and are in their own little classroom. What you'll find is in the schools that we'll visit they've got ... it's called *Leerkracht* ... L-E-E-R-K-R-A-C-H-T, literally *learning power* [Andre's emphasis], *Leer* is learn, *Kracht* is power, and it's the Dutch word for ... *Leerkracht* is a teacher in primary school. But literally it's a very powerful ... learning power. It's, I think, a foundation in the Netherlands ...[4]

[...]

Yeah, so every Monday; let's say every Monday a group of teachers comes together, not the ... whole school, but let's say six, or seven, or eight teachers; and they talk about what will be our aims for this week – and they negotiate about that and they write it down. So you visualise it. They look at what went on last week. They try to include student feedback, what did the children say, what information do we still need from the children? They organise school visits, and not school visits like inspection visits but 'Okay, can you give me some feedback on this and this and that, that?' And I think if you would have to summarise the secret of successful professional learning it is to de-privatise practices, teacher practices.

From her experiences with Montessori and her reading of Hattie, Anke had the courage to allow her teachers the freedom to develop the curriculum, and themselves, as they saw fit. This was to enable bottom-up growth within a hierarchical context. Indeed, Anke deliberately selected the teachers who were most resistant to change to be in the vanguard. For Anke, this meant that she had to support teachers whose pedagogic views were a mismatch with her own – but the teaching staff truly took ownership. One can witness this ownership walking around Emmaus school and it is not an uncommon sight to see several teachers gathered around a whiteboard discussing the curriculum – planning activities and changes. Such a sight – a demonstration of *Leerkracht* – is also evident within the Maria school in Rotterdam when I am shown around by the Principal, Judith van Wijngaarden:

AL: So could you maybe tell us a bit about learning power and how did you get involved with that?

JUDITH: The learning power because ... four years of top-down pushing the team to work I asked them what do you want to have from next ... what next step do you want to make? Yes, we want to work on the culture; we don't like the culture where we are working.

AL: Is that what the staff said?

JUDITH: The team, all the teachers say to me ... I say, 'Okay, I don't know how to change that but I want to look outside' and then I met Jaap from –

ANDRE: He's one of the architects of this –

JUDITH: He talked about his programme and I think, 'Ah, that's ... that's the next step for the team.' So I presented to the team and the teachers who have the most resistance about the principle. There was always resistance in the team, 'Yes, we want learning power.' So they ... I formed ... the Start Team with teachers with the most resistance; and they took ownership and they are my mirror because they want ... they can say what they want to have to change, and I reflect on my own behaviour, and I have to change to give them the trust to do the good things. To have the faith; that is the way we can make the next step, the next level in the school.

AL: So you deliberately chose the teachers who you knew were the most resistant?

JUDITH: Yes.

[...]

JUDITH: And now the next step we want to make is the ... transformative school ... is the Professor of the University of Amsterdam, I think, yes. We want to make a programme ... in the school because there is not only a problem from child, school and home; but child, school, home and street – and we want to put the street influence out of the children to put them higher on the educational ladder.

ANDRE: Trajectory kind of.

JUDITH: Yes, because the expectation of the streets are low; it's not good to do your ... best at school; and he is going to help us and the teachers to do the right things ... to give more trust and more power to the children. To challenge the street.

AL: So, that must mean then the teachers are going to have to leave the school building and actually go into the community – if they're going to address the problems of the street, as you call them?

JUDITH: Yes.

AL: So that's your next project?

JUDITH: That's the next project, yes. [Laughter]

Judith and her staff will need faith as they set themselves the highly ambitious target of confronting 'the street'. Iliass El Hadioui is the professor at Erasmus University, Rotterdam who studies the relationship between street and school culture and is the academic to whom Judith refers. His influence is to be found elsewhere in the port city of Rotterdam including ...

AL: So, we're in the streets of Rotterdam and I'm sitting here (in a café) with Sandra Groeneboom-Veelenturf who is the Director of Hildegardis School. So, would you like to just tell us something about your school please?

SANDRA: Our school has about 270-280 children and they are from very mixed culture background. Most of them are from Islam, Muslim children, 50-60% Moroccan, from Berber and then well about 30 Turkish and then some from ... Eastern Europe and from Sudan and Kurdistan.

AL: What are the challenges of your school then, what do you ...?

SANDRA: Mission, my mission is to get the children there, where they are supposed to be – from their intelligence and not from their background. So I think we have a strong mission to teach them in the eight years we have; to teach them where they are lacking of. So we see that they are poor in languages and so ... I have extension of time, 3 hours a week; so all children in the Netherlands go to school for about 24½ hours a week. My children are going 27½ hours a week to school and the 3 hours we have extra we put it in language. Language in all kinds of things, so also the language in maths, vocabulary and the understanding of reading.

AL: Can I ask how do the parents react to the fact their children are in school an extra 3 hours, are they quite comfortable with that or ...?

SANDRA: Yeah. Yeah. Yeah. I think it's in ... in Rotterdam we can all apply to extension of learning hours. All schools do that, or a lot of schools, especially in schools in the environments that we have. But you have a choice how you –

ANDRE: What you do with those hours.

SANDRA: What you do with those hours; and so you can fly in art people, or musicians, or ... I don't do that, my choice is that we ... the whole amount that I get from the council from Rotterdam, I put in extra teachers. So, I get about 135,000 euros a year extra and I can choose whether I get a teacher to come in and give music lessons ... [or] there is a teacher who gives art lessons; there are teachers who give gymnastics ... So the 120 hours there are people who are giving lessons; and the lessons that we have extra are put in languages and it pays off. I have a high ... comparing the same schools. So if you ...

ANDRE: They go to higher levels than –

SANDRA: Yes, they go to higher levels.

ANDRE: ... and your school does better than what is expected.

SANDRA: Yeah. For my children.

AL: Okay, is that just down to the extra 3 hours or ... there must be more to it than that?

SANDRA: [...] the other thing is we put a lot of effort in our climate in school ... but it's like something that breeds around the whole school. We have –

AL: Has it got a name?

SANDRA: Peaceful School ... the Peaceful School is about giving the children choices and giving them responsibility. Your responsibility for your behaviour, if you are ... if you misbehave there are responsibilities for that and not everyone has the same escapes.

[...]

AL: So, when you went to Hildegardis School, what was in your head, like what were your plans and ambitions for the school?

SANDRA: Well, I wanted to be a part of the community ... of course there are a lot of environmental things that are ... they influence the child and there is a lot of poorness in my neighbourhood; and children are walking the street until 11 o'clock in the evening; and they have parents who can't help with their homework or bring some structure in their lives. But our school is very structured, everything ... they know ... they know what their possibility is ... I think it's ... very important that ... you believe in them and that we are equally as good as the ... neighbourhood ... the district nearby who is really, really, rich. We can do it also, so we are a little bit competitive I think.

Strangely, similarities can be drawn between England's Academy Trusts and the Netherlands' form of schooling as depicted above e.g. longer school days, emphasis upon discipline and a desire to be competitive with schools sited in areas of higher socio-economic status. As discussed by Anke and Judith though, their approach to evidence-based practices through *Leerkracht* is somewhat looser; and Sandra also outlines how *Leerkracht* operates within her school:

SANDRA: ... And so we are trying to find out how to do that; but it's not me who's doing that. I have groups, working groups and every teacher is in one group and they can choose one of the groups by interest and ability when they are ... I believe if you put your teacher in strength and they can do things they are good at, then it's nice to work. So we ... I have all kinds of groups. They have to be in one, you can't say you're not going in one, you have to go in one. And they ... do professional things together, look in other schools where they have already developed some of the things they are searching for; or they go on a work-shop and then all the things they learn that go ... on the learning power board; or we have ... meetings where ... we call it 'boundary crossing' - where they take their knowledge that they learnt outside into the school. And then after they ... have explained what they have learnt; we decide together whether we put it on the learning board - or whether it's just inspiration - or whether it's something we would like to develop further. And that's really powerful because you have a lot of commitment when you decide together, if you want to go on a new path. So ...

AL: So, you're really relying on the teachers' professional judgement; they're saying, 'We went to visit this school and we were impressed by what we found and we think it could work here, or we're not sure if it could work here, what do you think?' And you ask the other teachers and say, 'What do you think?'

SANDRA: Yes, and there is maybe somebody who went to a workshop - or have learnt by reading an article; and they talk about it and then they specialise it. When we think together it's a really important issue, we put it on the board.

AL: And sometimes you don't ... sometimes you say, 'No, it's not for us'?

SANDRA: Yeah. Yeah, because they called me 'the red Ferrari' when I came; because they thought I was going way too fast, way too fast and so ... I've noticed that if you want things because you know it's ... for the best then it doesn't work. It's not working. You have to have commitment of the group for something to work. Of course you can arrange ... you can ... influence the way you go; but I think it's really powerful if you do it together.

AL: To collaborate together?

SANDRA: Yes. Yeah.

There is an interesting comparison to be drawn here with Bawtry Mayflower primary school. At Bawtry, the staff were required to undertake an evidence-based project as one of their four appraisal targets and this resulted in a variety of different topics being researched. This approach was individualised although sometimes teachers worked in pairs. Bawtry has since moved to a Disciplined Inquiry Approach whereby all of the staff form one professional com-munity as they research the same topic. However, with *Leerkracht*, there are several pro-fessional communities within each of the Emmaus, Maria and Hildegardis' schools and the staff have more freedom to select their topics for experimentation and innovation. Further, there seems to be more allowance for teachers to progress at their own pace - even if some may appear to be at 'Dead Slow'! The schools in England have an advantage, though, when it comes to quality of the research - especially, if they are a member of a research school or a

Multi-Academy Trust: there is a close-to-hand and wider forum for dissemination, sharing and collaboration. Additionally, they have access to the expertise of good offices of such as the EEF, the Centre for the Use of Research and Evidence in Education (CUREE), researchED, etc.

However, Sandra then outlines a collaborative role within the community that is quite distinctive and that she terms as a 'pedagogic community district vision':

AL: Can you explain a wee bit more about … you said about the school and the community?

SANDRA: Yes. Yes.

AL: What's your thinking there?

SANDRA: I think you can't do it on your own and the children go outside and they play outside; and we really like that the children behave as they behave within the school time – they behave the same way equally outside of school and that is a real challenge. So … what we did is we … we wrote a *pedagogic community district vision*. I don't know if that's the word but we sat down with all the network partners and we thought about, 'Well, what do we think are the values of this like district, this community?' So, I can show you I have it here. We made … we talked about it with … about 30 different network partners. So, everything you can think of, also for the old people, for the poor people, for the homeless people; they all sit together – policemen, schools, everybody and we made our own four values of the community.

AL: So that's autonomy, respect, creativity and positivity? [recalling from pamphlet]

SANDRA: Yes! That's it and when we made this we also said well … what do the children need to do? What do they … how do we have to act? … So what do we expect from 4 year olds, what do we expect from 12 years old and what do we expect from 18 years old? And at the other side it's … what does it ask from the people who are working with these children? What do they have to have, like abilities to work together?

AL: Is this teachers and policemen, social workers, shop workers?

SANDRA: Everyone, yes but also the people from the elderly home, I don't know what –

AL: So, well, yeah; so if I went into an elderly home, right, would I see this? Would this be somewhere within the home?

SANDRA: Well we have … this we've made some … it's brand new, we have made some big signs and in every public … on every public building they are putting these signs on.

AL: Really!

SANDRA: And we have made an animation film and the animation film is where we explain the four visions of the community; and so, if you are new in the community you will see it on every website. But I also show it to new parents what we expect in this neighbourhood …

The concept of a community school is a familiar term within the UK – but the idea and practice that a school should be the main agent in establishing community values is unusual. In a later chapter we learn that there is a concern of middle class teachers being divorced from the lives of the working class communities that they serve. Sandra's model of a *pedagogic community district vision* partially addresses this. I presume that it derives from the school's association with Erasmus University's professor Hadioui; but it may also be influenced by the presence of Gert Biesta on the RVKO board – and his work we shall now briefly consider.

Values critique

> professional judgements in education are ultimately value judgements,
> not simply technical judgements.

(Biesta 2007)

To some extent, this chapter is a Dutch critique – both professional and academic – of evidence-based practices. It is Dutch and professional in that it draws upon two visits to Rotterdam and professional conversations with both Andre Koffeman and the aforementioned three primary school head teachers: Anke; Judith; and Sandra. It is Dutch and academic in that it now considers the influential paper 'Why 'what works' won't work' (2007) by the renowned Rotterdam-born educationist, Gert Biesta. As can be surmised, an approach to education based upon evidence-based practices is not without its critics. Biesta (2007) succinctly summarises the criticisms of opponents as follows:

[1]   … question[ing] the homology between education and medicine …

[2]   … question[ing] the positivistic assumptions underlying the idea of evidence-based education …

[3]   … criticis[ing] the managerial agenda of evidence-based education …

[4]   … object[ing] to the lack of an acknowledgment of the crucial role of values in educational research and practice.

- In Chapter 9 we look at the devastating critique of education research by David Hargreaves who compares it unfavourably with the world of medicine;
- drawing upon the work of Wilfred Carr, Chapter 3 examines the instrumental nature of classroom life and the empiricist approach to education; and there is further consideration afforded to this in Chapter 8;
- both Chapters 9 and 10 afford a strategic overview of evidence-based approaches to education; and so
- in this chapter we acknowledge 'the crucial role of values'.

Biesta (2007) contends that 'education is at heart a moral practice more than a technological enterprise'. To illuminate, he cites the example proffered by David Carr whereby we have 'conclusive empirical evidence that in all cases physical punishment is the most effective way of deterring or controlling disruptive behaviour'. This may be so; but such action is morally reprehensible. Since both the means and the ends of education are constitutively interrelated then education is more about what is educationally *desirable* rather than what is educationally *possible*. Indeed, classroom pedagogy entails a host of judgements and philosophically it is more akin to *practical wisdom* than *instrumental knowledge* (Biesta, 2007). With the latter there is an inherent danger of Stenhouse's 'teacher as intellectual navvy' if teachers *base* their actions on the evidence that has been sought and determined elsewhere by others. Rather, teachers should exercise judgement whereby their actions are *informed* by evidences. This nuanced distinction between evidence-based and evidence-informed practices is supported by education theorist-practitioners such as Philippa Cordingley, Chief Executive of CUREE (see Chapter 9).

However, on the final evening of this most enjoyable professional excursion and skimming the murky, surface waters on the high-speed boat back to the *SS Rotterdam*, thoughts turn to those most heavily invested with evidence-based practices: research schools. It is time to dive deeper.

Notes

1   For readers unfamiliar with the Dutch education system, brief descriptions can be found at www. nuffic.nl/en/subjects/education-in-the-netherlands/ and https://en.wikipedia.org/wiki/Education_in_ the_Netherlands
2   RVKO comprises 66 primary schools and 20 playgroups in Rotterdam and surrounding areas.
3   Senior lecturer at Amsterdam University of the Applied Sciences who acted as an 'interpreter' for the professional conversations in Rotterdam.
4   See https://hundred.org/en/innovations/leerkracht

References

Biesta, G. 2007. Why 'what works' won't work: evidence-based practice and the democratic deficit in educational research. *Educational Theory* 57(1) 1-22. Available from: https://onlinelibrary.wiley.com/doi/full/10.1111/j.1741-5446.2006.00241.x [Accessed 9 November 2019]
Carr, W. 1986. Theories of theory and practice. *Journal of Philosophy of Education* 20(2) 177-186.
Hattie, J. 2012. *Visible Learning for Teachers: Maximizing Impact on Learning*. Abingdon, Oxon: Routledge.
The Holy Bible. New Revised Standard Version. 2005. Catholic edition. London: Darton, Longman & Todd.

7 Deep diving
Research schooling

People are too quick and the deep dives aren't deep enough.
(James Siddle, Director of Kyra Research School, 3 May 2019)

Introduction

In November 2010, then secretary of State for Education, Michael Gove, taking a lead from the 'Race to the Top' initiative in the USA announced his intention to set up an education endowment foundation that would help to raise standards of attainment in schools sited in challenging areas of socio-economic deprivation. The following year witnessed the creation of the Education Endowment Foundation (EEF) by the Sutton Trust – a charity with the laudable mission to 'fight for social mobility from birth to the workplace so that every young person – no matter … what school they go to, or where they live – has the chance to succeed in life' (www.suttontrust.com/about-us/).

With the benefit of a £125 million grant from the Department of Education a formal launch of the EEF took place in July 2011. According to the chairman, Sir Peter Lampl (2011), the EEF is:

> an exciting and hugely significant development … This will be used to develop initiatives to raise the attainment of the poorest pupils in the most challenging schools. Crucially, it has a 15-year time horizon to evaluate what works, both in the immediate and long term, free from political pressures.

There can be little doubt that, since its inception, the EEF has made a significant impact and as attested in its 2018 annual report it has commissioned 160 trials 'involving more than 10,000 schools … and reaching well over one million children and young people' (EEF, 2018:2).[1] Indeed, *The Economist* (2018) no less, makes the bold claim that the EEF 'has turned the English school system into a giant test-bed'. That said, the same magazine points out that: 'the EEF has come to the realisation that the 'passive presentation of evidence is not enough' … [and] results published last year found that providing schools with high quality evidence about teaching led to no improvement with pupils' performance' (*The Economist*, 2018). Perhaps this disappointment led to the birth of the Research Schools Network which is a collaboration between the EEF and the Institute for Effective Education (IEE) to create a schools' network that will enhance the use of evidence-based practices to improve teaching.

At present, there are 32 research schools that act as regional hubs for the network. Through the Research Schools Network these schools share knowledge about putting research into practice, and they assist schools to render their classroom pedagogies more evidence informed.

Acting as a regional hub the research schools work with other schools to:

- encourage schools to make use of evidence-based programmes and practices through regular communication and events;
- provide training and professional development for senior leaders and teachers on how to improve classroom practice based on the best available evidence; and
- support schools to develop innovative ways of improving teaching and learning and providing them with the expertise to evaluate their impact.

(https://the-iee.org.uk/what-we-do/research-schools-network/)

This Research Schools Network is set to expand further and even, at present, it makes challenging demands of some staff (see below) who take up posts referred to as Strategic Research Leads (SRL) or Evidence Leads in Education (ELE) or such like.

Wednesday, 1 May 2019

St Margaret's Church of England primary school, Withern, near Alford, Lincolnshire

Professional conversation with James Siddle, Head Teacher and Director of Kyra Research School

AL: I was speaking to Julie at Doncaster Research School, they've got these like Strategic Research Leads ... with a specific function in certain schools to raise awareness of research; do you have anything similar at Kyra?

JAMES: Yeah. Yeah. Yeah. In fact, we've probably got a more developed model in that we've done it for longer; we have what we called ELEs. So, Evidence Leads in Education which the EEF have now picked up on and now they're rolling out a model nationwide. So we developed a model of ... because the East Midlands is geographically so large we felt that we couldn't cover all the bases. Driving across Lincolnshire takes you two hours, so we've got a Hub Research School now in Leicestershire. The EEF have picked up on that and they're now developing an associate research school; so the network is increasing. There's going to be another ten actual research schools and then there will be associate research schools [that] will be affiliated to research schools and – ...

AL: What do they do, what does an Evidence Lead? ...

JAMES: A variety of things; so we've got an Evidence Lead here in my school. So the things that she's done recently ... so she led a session with head teachers on Knowledge-Based Curriculum, on things like Cognitive Theory and the Science of Learning. So, what does the evidence suggest about retrieval practice, about interleaving-based theory, dual coding theory? So, she's done presentations on them as well.

At a practical level concerning the geographical spread of schools this development of hub research schools/associate research schools is to be welcomed. However, it is worth pausing and reflecting upon the level of knowledge and expertise expected of SRLs or ELEs. To lead the three sessions listed above and to be knowledgeable about the three theories is demanding; and it poses a fundamental question about the degree of expertise that can reasonably be expected of teachers with lead responsibilities for research. Indeed, this is the essence of a critique posed by Nutt (2018) in his piece, 'Research schools are stuck in a quagmire' in the *Times Education Supplement*. He contends that: 'The onus has fallen on sincere, professional teachers with minimal research experience but bags of goodwill, to try and accumulate the considerable skills and experience needed, as best they can.' And Nutt cites two examples of what he terms 'murky holes' that can confront an ELE or SRL:

1. *A form of self-citation*. Drawing upon a report from the Department for International Development (DfID) and its ten ethical principles for research and evaluation, he cites the ninth i.e. *research and evaluation should usually be independent of those implementing an intervention or programme under study*. Applying this recommendation Nutt (2018) criticises a 35-page research report on social mobility commissioned by the EEF that 'happily cites research by the EEF's parent funder, The Sutton Trust, no less than 10 times'. He goes as far as to talk of 'deceit', 'unabashed zealotry' and 'research ... [being] commissioned by a member of the faithful'. Further, he even claims that 'this inces-tuous use of "evidence" is common'. These are strong allegations. Many commentators, myself included, would counter that given the trustworthiness of the Sutton Trust and the EEF with regard to social mobility, Nutt's criticism and language are unwar-ranted. Nonetheless, as presented, this is a 'murky hole' that should be avoided by ELE s and SRLs.
2. *Obfuscation*. A more valid criticism is when Nutt (2018) condemns 'obfuscation' and cites an example of a researcher hiding the inadequacy of their understanding and use of the term 'effect size' within the footnotes. He also cites a second example of obfuscation with respect to a report from the Organisation for Economic Cooperation and Development (OECD). His criticisms are sufficient to affirm his concern that teachers with responsibility as a Research Lead will be required to develop a *'sophisticated research literacy'* that some might argue is beyond their job remit.

With respect to *research literacy* the British Educational Research Association (BERA) gives a steer. In 2014, in conjunction with the RSA (Royal Society for the encouragement of Arts, manufactures and commerce) they published a report titled *Research and the Teaching Profession*. In appendix 2 they explain their terminology and five of these are worthy of repro-ducing here, almost in their entirety.

The first of these is *enquiry-based learning* which they describe as action research or enquiry-based practice. Practitioner enquiry (inquiry) may be a better descriptive term than the latter but, in any case, both 'action research' and 'practitioner enquiry' have a rich history within the world of education. However, because such action research studies and practi-tioner enquiries are so context-specific, they are accorded a low esteem within the world of education research. Indeed, I recall at one of the meetings for the Education sub-unit for the 2014 Research Excellence Framework (REF) several of the senior academics were reluctant to accept such research activities as 'proper research'. For academic researchers the gold standard is generalisability and this is neither a feature of practitioner enquiry nor a concern for teachers.

The second term is *research literacy* which BER (2014) depicts as a familiarity with a range of research methods and an understanding of the implications of the latest research findings for not only day-to-day practice; but also the broader field of education policy. Inherent within research literacy is a critical appreciation of the limitations of research. It may not be necessary for teachers and school leaders to have studied at Masters and Doctorate levels in order to be deemed as research literate; but it would seem that some level of study would be appropriate and helpful. Certainly, in recent years, the research component within undergraduate study for trainee teachers has increased and so, within the early years of their profession, many newly qualified teachers (NQTs) and recently qualified teachers (RQTs) can be held to be research literate. Whether that suffices to take up a post as a Strategic Research Lead or Evidence Lead in Education is a moot point.

Their third research term is *research engaged* and this refers to actually undertaking research. Such active participation with research may take many forms up to and including the 'gold standard' of randomised control trials (RCTs). One would hope that schools which are so engaged would have a high degree of competency, if not expertise, in educational research. Such a term encompasses a wide spectrum of agency. The Disciplined Inquiry Approach by Bawtry Mayflower primary school (discussed in Chapter 4) falls within the category of in-depth analysis of school performance data – and this entails an active, knowledgeable approach by school staff. Participation with a RCT, though, may be more passive and usually entails an association with the EEF or a university department.

The penultimate term employed by the authors of the BERA (2014: 40) report is *research-rich* and this refers to 'environments, usually schools and colleges, in which research thrives. Research-rich schools and colleges encourage innovation, creativity and enquiry-based practice, enabling teachers and leaders to drive change, rather than have it "done" to them.' This would seem to be an apt description for a research school. Reflecting upon the BERA terms one can postulate that:

- all teachers, at some points in their career, should undertake enquiry-based learning understood as action research or practitioner enquiry;
- most, if not all teachers should be research literate and develop a critical appreciation and understanding of education research;
- all schools are research engaged with respect to school performance data – and all schools should, at some point, become research engaged with universities, the EEF or similar organisations such as IEE, CUREE, etc.; and
- research schools should distinguish themselves as being a research-rich environment in which they promote and encourage other education institutions to become likewise.

With such thoughts swirling in the background, before moving on to the fifth research term I continue the professional conversation with James Siddle; and it soon becomes apparent that whilst the above aspiration is a 'wish-list', 'baby steps' are being taken towards its realisation:

AL: So, is it really at an awareness raising stage at the minute, raising issues, raising problems, raising good practice?

JAMES: ... This week she's [Evidence Lead Education] been working with a Multi-Academy Trust they wanted to ... they've kind of looked at ... broadly at the research evidence and they've decided that the feedback and marking is something they wanted to focus on. They wanted to know what was the evidence base and where do they start across the Multi-Academy Trust. So, she went down and sort of looked at the evidence with ... interestingly, when she came back she said, 'Well, their main focus seemed to be feedback and marking is about what teachers do, it's about books, it's about what we put in books.' And I think she, through the evidence, not through her own opinion, sort of turned that on its head a bit and said, 'Well, actually, you need to start with the pupils, starting thinking about it in slightly different ways.' And, again, they were thinking about, 'Well, I must have pupils having targets, we must give them half-termly targets; but what's the evidence for half-termly targets?' You know and again just ... fairly rich conversations around well, 'Why do you think this?' And again, it comes back to, I think, the Ofsted inspectors are going to come in and go up to a child and say 'What's your target?' and they must be able to regurgitate and understand what their target is et cetera. So the motivation is there, the start points that aren't the start points that you were hoping to have – as opposed to what does the evidence suggest about use of target setting, success criteria, et cetera.

This takes us back to the opening quote of this chapter i.e. 'People are too quick and the deep dives aren't deep enough.' After a broad survey of the research evidence, the Multi-Academy Trust (MAT) is seeking a quick fix regarding feedback and marking – specifically with respect to target setting. But they are being recommended to 'dive deeper' and to ask of themselves – what does the evidence say with regard to the value of marking and setting targets?[2] However, the fact that the MAT is looking at research evidence and seeking expert support is a step forward:

AL: Okay, so how would you say the overall picture looks compared to say three years ago?
JAMES: I would say that ... yeah ... very different as in the conversations are very different, the fact that the Multi-Academy Trust can come to us and say, 'We know we have to do ... we think the evidence suggests that feedback, marking is going to have a significant difference.' I mean, even that to me when I first started, it was very much who had the loudest voice in the staffroom. 'I've been doing this for X number of years, we need to do this.' You know, you're thinking, 'Well, why? Why do you need to do this?' I remember going out to schools thinking what does outstanding practice really look like; because I don't really know. But now actually there are ... the conversations are different. The sources of evidence are there apparently, it's just how we actually delve into it; and I think we're at that stage where people are having those kinds of ... we know that we should be doing this; but I still don't think the people know quite how to do it. So for example, the ELE again, when they were talking about feedback and marking it just seemed huge.
[...]
JAMES: Everything seemed huge, the evidence base, where do we even start with all this? There are all these research papers et cetera. How do we possibly do this? Especially when the impetus for change is often rapid; when, actually, what you need to do is actually take your time to actually delve into it; and the weakest area for me still is the amount of time that people spend looking into the evidence base. *People are too quick and the deep dives aren't deep enough* [emphasis added].

As with the earlier discussion with Julie and Claire of Bawtry Mayflower school – on the one hand, there are times when a 'quick fix' is appropriate – perhaps to prepare for an upcoming Ofsted inspection. On the other hand, though, there are too many 'quick fixes' and 'sticking plasters' – a lot of educational change is not thought through thoroughly. And that is through pressure – from data findings, Ofsted forebodings:

AL: So they're just rushing into it?

JAMES: Yeah.

AL: Because that's what they're used to doing?

JAMES: Yes. Yeah and … that's what the system as well demands: rapid change. If you're in a pickle, in terms of your school, there is rapid change needed. And rapid change isn't necessarily sustainable, it isn't necessarily in accordance with the evidence base. I think there are some real positive moves from Ofsted; but I think sometimes there are gaps in the evidence as well and we're pushing again. So, for example, you look at the new Ofsted framework; what we've been exposed to so far; and it talks about doing space practice. But actually space learning is different from distributed theory and there is confusion there. What space practice or distributed theory looks like for a 4 year old child compared to a 14 year old child learning a vocabulary item, we don't know. The evidence isn't actually out there; and actually what you can end up doing is more harm than good. So, actually, you're always pushed somewhere. You have to be seen to do something; but actually is the evidence strong enough to suggest what you should do in a small rural school for a 4 year old child? Maybe that's not there. So … it's … it's a bit of a minefield sometimes; and you're pushed and pulled in different directions which aren't always educationally sound.

AL: I'm thinking about what you're saying because I was speaking with Julie Jenkinson, the head teacher at Bawtry and her and her … the Research Lead is Claire Dunn and they've always had a history of research … and targets, one a year; and they had to do something in research. So, because of that I did some work with them and gave them a kind of higher profile; and they're now involved at various levels with Doncaster Research School. So they're much more aware of research. She made an interesting point about her School Development Plan, that she is quite prepared to sit and wait. Just what you were saying people are not doing, she actually brought this up. She said, 'Well, I'm much more prepared to say it's not going to happen this year. It's going to happen the year after; we're going to spend this time investigating and looking because I really want to embed this. It's worthwhile, it needs time but we have to investigate properly' – and that's a change I haven't seen before because normally you're right, there's rapid change, quick response –

JAMES: Yeah, we'll do this this year, this next year.

AL: And she's even prepared … she agrees with you about quick fixes. Sometimes you have to find a quick fix because Ofsted will come in or they'll just arrive; but she said even if Ofsted came she would be quite happy to say, 'Well, we're still investigating this. I realise there's an issue but we're taking our time to find out the evidence.'

It takes a degree of courage to think and plan long-term and to, a certain extent, set aside concerns about Ofsted. We saw this in previous chapters with head teachers, Julie Jenkinson and Chris Wilson, at Bawtry Mayflower and Ramsden primary schools. It also involves a 'marriage' between what is happening at the chalk-face and what can be gleaned from research evidences. This calls to mind the final research term used in the BERA report i.e. *research informed clinical practice*. Such practice necessitates the collation of knowledge and evidence from different sources and through a carefully designed programme this aims to 'integrate teachers' experiential learning at the "chalk-face" with research-based knowledge and insights from academic study and scholarship' (BERA, 2014: 41).

In our professional conversation, James then discusses what may be termed, loosely, as a 'case study' of *research informed educational practice* with respect to inference and vocabulary. It affords an insight to the complexity and long-term nature of such change:

JAMES: And producing sustained change, again so it's doing things too quickly sometimes; but then sustaining it over a period of time is a massive change. So, I can give an example from my own school where about 2–3 years ago we looked at the data; and the data suggested that pupils weren't doing as well on inference questions, it's a common issue. So, we looked into the research around inference. One of the things that it flagged up was that if they didn't understand a text through lack of vocabulary then they couldn't understand … they weren't able to gain the inference from it. So … so … we also looked at the discrete inference items, vocabulary items and they weren't doing very well on that. So the data married up, so we looked at …

We spent a good six months just delving into what the research said on explicit vocabulary instruction. Looked into the CPD around it, around how to support it, looked at the implementation guidance et cetera. Became really interested in instructional coaching as a model. So we put in place, I put it in place in three schools, [with] the two partner schools at the same time.

AL: Who are these two partners?

JAMES: Stickney Primary and New Leake, so they're … I used to work at Stickney. So we've still got strong links.

AL: Just like an informal –

JAMES: Yeah. Yeah. We just worked with them for a period of years … So we started off in September here, Monday morning introducing the vocabulary item. Everyone had a coach and we spent 6–8 weeks; the evidence suggested a sustained period of time for something of medium complexity in terms of … pedagogical approach. Six to eight weeks to support each other, just for that first 15 minutes of how to introduce the vocabulary item. And after about 8 weeks we all agreed that we felt we'd got it. So it took us up to Christmas, we had a couple of weeks' break after Christmas. We then looked at how you do the various items to delve deeper into the meanings of the words. So, kind of Monday, Tuesday, Wednesday we did the instructional coaching through that; and then I kind of felt after Easter that I put my teachers under a bit of pressure because everyone had a coach every single week coming in for 15 minutes. I thought well I'll relax it; everyone is doing it. I'll take it out for the assessment bit. That would have been the final bit; and I pulled it out and everyone just stopped teaching it.

So … everybody agreed that they agreed with the research, everybody was doing it; but as soon as I pulled it out in terms of that accountability measure, the other two schools they didn't put instruction coaching in at all: and it disappeared within half a term. One or two teachers here or there were doing it but nobody else ... so what I had to do the following September was put it back in again; and put it in for another whole half term but now it's happening again. Interestingly, it happens routinely as part of ... actually what we had to do with that was the equivalent of a whole year of supported instructional coaching. Every staff meeting to start with we were working with the coach for 15 minutes. Everyone would have a little video to watch et cetera. But even after two terms when everyone agreed, everyone ... the evidence suggests that you should make sure they understand the research evidence beforehand so they connect to it ... but then if you have an accountability system, even if you have got conscripts rather than volunteers you can still get them; but after two terms it went.

So that's a challenge in itself; what's good practice, sustaining it. I often look at School Development Plans – people often send me things. I just look at them and go 'It's not going to happen.' You just see it on paper because it's not implemented, it's not evaluated; those two things aren't dovetailed. Implementation and evaluation, even if you look at the EEF stuff they have ... they ... what is a logic model they've called it an Implementation Plan. But one of the strengths of an Implementation Plan or a logic model is its simplicity; but it's also one of its weaknesses because it's not fundamentally about evaluation. It's about implementation. It might tell you some measures in there but it doesn't tell you how you're going to go about them. It doesn't tell you about workload, about who's got to create the survey, who's going to analyse it, when are they going to give it back? What if there's a problem with what's come out of the survey? None of that is in there. So even the models that are being given aren't sustainable in terms of evaluation. *So that's another ... complexity that's out there in the system; but again the complexity doesn't lend itself for short termism* [emphasis added].

Complexity of evidence-based practices

It seems that the more one delves into evidence-based practices (EBP) then the more complicated it becomes. James Siddle is highly knowledgeable with respect to EBP and RCTs in particular – and he is adept at garnering support for EBP projects. However, even he acknowledges the complexity of the system. At this juncture, it is good to recall the earlier comment of EEF chairman, Sir Peter Lampl, that the Education Endowment Foundation has a 15-year time horizon. But, given that he spoke of this nine years ago, 2026 does not seem that far away. It is also worthy of note that the Research Schools Network is expanding with ten new schools and seven associate research schools being created (Ward, 2019a): but will this suffice? Sir Kevan Collins, then CEO of the EEF claims that:

> We're at an important moment in the potential of evidence to improve teaching and learning in England's schools, particularly for our most disadvantaged young people. Not only is this country now a world-leader in producing high-quality evidence, but there is also a large and growing appetite among teachers and senior leaders to use this research to underpin their school's improvement.

> (Ward 2019b)

It is difficult to argue against this. The Royal County of Berkshire hosts the National Foundation for Education Research (NFER) that was established in 1946 as a centre for educational research and development in England and Wales.[3] The West Midlands is home to the established and renowned Centre for the Use of Research and Evidence in Education (CUREE). From this Coventry base they:

- conduct research reviews and syntheses of practitioner enquiries and academic research;
- downscale large-scale research for practitioners through the use of interactive tools, protocols and resources;
- undertake policy analysis and development; and
- offer various modes of continuous professional development.

Meanwhile, in the gothic city of York is to be found the Institute for Effective Education (IEE) that lists amongst its aims:

- help teachers and schools reflect on their practice to identify the challenges they face;
- ... help schools to develop and evaluate new approaches that build on ... evidence;
- find new ways of connecting research with practice.

(https://the-iee.org.uk/who-we-are/our-aims/)

The international, UK capital city of London boasts the Chartered College of Teaching, the Teacher Development Trust, the Evidence for Policy and Practice Information (EPPI) Co-ordinating Centre (https://eppi.ioe.ac.uk/cms/); and the phenomenon that is researchED. As an influential newcomer on the educational scene the Chartered College of Teaching (CCoT) has a vision that: 'Teachers are working in the most effective, *informed way* [emphasis added] to provide the best possible education for children and young people now, and in the future.' And by 'informed' the CCoT intends to:

- be the conduit to a more evidence-informed profession; and
- provide access to professional knowledge and intellectual challenge.

(https://chartered.college/vision-and-mission)

Founded by teachers in London in March 2012, the Teacher Development Trust is a UK charity whose approach is that of 'supporting world class, evidence-informed professional learning' (https://tdtrust.org/about/mission). The following year saw the birth of researchED which is:

a grass-roots, teacher led organization started ... by Tom Bennett ... [who] ... suggest[ed] on Twitter that he was putting together a conference on educational research, and did anyone want to help? Four hours later, by 2am, he had received two hundred offers of help, moral support, venues and volunteer speakers. 'I didn't build researchED,' says Tom, 'it wanted to be built. It built itself. I just ran with it.'

(https://researched.org.uk/about/our-story/)

The opening web page proclaims that it is now 'ResearchED – A Global Community' and this is backed up by its list of forthcoming research conferences (at time of writing) i.e.:

- Cape Town, South Africa;
- Dollar, Fife, Scotland;
- Dublin, Ireland;
- Ipswich, Northampton and Surrey, England;
- Santiago, Chile;
- Rome, Italy;
- Philadelphia, USA; and
- Cardiff, Wales.

Even the gritty, north-east city of Sunderland can lay claim to being the home of the Evidence Based Education network (https://evidencebased.education) and luminaries such as professor Rob Coe.

This is a mightily impressive, and not exhaustive list in support of Collins's claim above that England's education system is world-leading with regard to producing high-quality evidence.

Moreover, there is little doubt that there is a 'growing appetite among teachers and senior leaders to use this research to underpin their school's improvement'. This is evidenced by the list above and the growing Research Schools Network. And yet, and yet ... it still seems that there is a long way to go. The more that a teacher, a school, a MAT, a local authority involves itself with research – the more complex that the picture becomes. Does this mean that one shouldn't bother as it is too complicated? No. Taking a lead from Aristotle's (2018) classic work *Metaphysics*:

> For it is an advantage to advance to that which is more knowable. For learning proceeds for all in this way – through that which is less knowable by nature to that which is more knowable ... Now what is knowable and primary for particular sets of people is often knowable to a very small extent ... But yet one must start from that which is barely knowable but knowable to oneself, and try to know what is knowable without qualification.

Aristotle encourages us to believe that all things are knowable – which is a highly debatable point – but, pragmatically, to acknowledge that in our journey towards complete knowledge, there will be times when we recognise that there are more things to learn. During this journey it will be helpful to have a path to follow: but which path?

Academia

Turning to academia – might this offer a solution? Fortuitously, this summer of 2019 saw the publication of a special issue of *Educational Research and Evaluation* titled 'The Evidential Basis of "Evidence-Based Education"'. There is a justified criticism that evidence-based education (EBE) is too closely associated with randomised controlled trials (RCTs) and their subsequent influence upon makers of education policy (Phillips, 2019; Simpson, 2019a). The usefulness of RCTs is further undermined by Joyce (2019: 43) who contends that 'claims regarding representativeness tend to be poorly evidenced'. Further criticisms levelled at EBE and RCTs are:

- claims that RCTS rank as rigorous evidence are misleading (Cartwright, 2019);
- EBE often lacks theoretical background that is necessary to interpret and understand the results of particular interventions and this undermines its relevance and usefulness to frontline professionals (Cowen, 2019);

- the use of effect sizes in EBE as a driver for policymaking in education is based on a false assumption and the guest editor of this journal (Simpson, 2019b) lambasts organisations such as the EEF for the alleged ineptitude of their response to criticisms; and
- Wrigley and McCusker (2019:110) 'examine the insistent claims by advocates of evidence-based teaching that it is a rigorous scientific approach ... [and] ... suggest these claims are often based on a rhetorical appeal ... and a failure to recognise the complexity of education and pedagogy'.

A 'saving grace' may be the paper by Kvernbekk (2019: 25) who, heeding the advice of Stenhouse (1980b) that researchers must justify themselves to practitioners, makes a case for 'RCT evidence and what their possible attraction for practitioners might be'. However, in his summation of this special issue of the journal, Wiliam (2019) inflicts a *coup de grâce* when he admonishes that 'the claims made for evidence-based education, and in particular the role that randomised control trials might play within such an approach, do not stand up to scrutiny even in their own terms'.

The main advocate of EBE and RCTs in the UK is, of course, the EEF; and when, previously, they suffered similar criticism in 2016, they have countered with a robust defence (e.g. Nevill, 2016). But the criticisms of education research are legion. Throughout a 40-year career in education there has never been a dearth of such criticism. It causes one to wonder if, perhaps, we are on the wrong path when it comes to understanding and improving educational practices. In an earlier chapter we discussed an *interpretative* approach to educational practice (see Figure 3.1). However, EBE has an *empirical* understanding of educational practice which advocates the scientific method of drawing a general conclusion or principle from a number of observed facts; and preferably through the use of RCTs.

However, with such an empirical approach to educational practice, power lies with the community of education researchers as they debate and determine *which* are the principles and *how* they should be applied in the classrooms. In the meantime, through an objectives/outcomes approach to educational practices, teachers are reduced to mere technicians and worse; as in the words of Lawrence Stenhouse (1980a: 5):

> the objectives model actually rests on an acceptance of the school teacher as a kind of intellectual navvy. An objectives-based curriculum is like a site plan simplified so that people know exactly where to dig their trenches without having to know why.

Such a prospect is unpalatable. A more professional, palatable option is the *interpretative* approach to educational practice. Herein the form of knowledge of educational practice is interpretative i.e. it is concerned with explaining the meaning of educational practices through both subjective and objective evidence. Classroom life is held to be essentially communicative in nature i.e. it is concerned with the exchange of information, ideas and feelings. And now the function of the teacher is practical, in that we consider these informed explanations of educational practice as a basis for our deliberations about what *ought* to be done in a particular situation (Carr, 1986). This is a richer, more nuanced description of educational practices. It accords more with the reality of classroom life. And as 'ought' implies – this communicative approach acknowledges that there is a moral dimension to the life of the classroom.

Aristotle

The roots of these two differing understandings of approaches to educational practice can be traced back to our Greek friend Aristotle: and his distinction between *technical reason* and *practical reason*. In his profound work, *Back to the Rough Ground: Practical Judgement and the Lure of Technique*, Joseph Dunne (1997) explores the distinctions between technical reason and practical reason; and he enlightens us through the writings of Aristotle in book 6 of the *Nichomachean Ethics*. On the one hand, we learn that the empirical, objectives/outcomes model of educational practice can be equated with *technê*. This is a kind of activity that involves 'making' or 'production' (*poiesis*) and which results 'in a durable outcome, a product or a state of affairs (a house, a goblet, a person restored to good health) which can be precisely specified by the maker before he engages in his activity' (Dunne, 1997: 9). These activities require technical reason.

On the other hand, we learn about practical reason:

> Besides *poiesis*, the activity of producing outcomes, [Aristotle] recognized another type of activity, *praxis*, which is conduct in a public space with others in which a person, without ulterior purpose and with a view to no object detachable from himself, acts in such a way as to realize excellences that he has come to appreciate in his community as constitutive of a worthwhile way of life ... As an activity that both involved one with other people and at the same time was a realization of one's self, praxis engaged one more intimately, or afforded one less detachment, than the poiesis over which [one] exercised an uncompromised sovereignty. And for this reason ... praxis required for its regulation a kind of knowledge that was more personal and experiential, more supple and less formulable, than the knowledge conferred by *technê*. This practical knowledge ... Aristotle called *phronesis*.
>
> (Dunne 1997: 10)

Quite simply, which is it to be? *Poiesis* or *praxis*? *Technê* or *phronesis*? Classroom teaching is not akin to the construction of a house, or the fashioning of a goblet, or restoration of health: and no teacher exercises 'uncompromised sovereignty'. On these grounds, this rules out poiesis and technê – and disavows technical reason. At its best, classroom teaching is a community in pursuit of excellence. Based on this aspiration, this is praxis and phronesis – and invites practical reason.

If, as argued above, classroom life is concerned with practical reason and not technical reason – then what of all the technical studies carried out by the EEF? Are they rendered useless? Not so. If we return to Wilfred Carr's description of the interpretative form of knowledge of educational practice i.e. it concerns itself with explaining the meaning of educational practices through *both subjective and objective evidence*. The role of the teacher, then, is to employ practical reason – and this entails consideration of informed explanations of educational practice (objective and subjective evidence) as a basis for our deliberations about what *ought* to be done in our classrooms.

And my lived classroom experiences corroborate this claim: classroom pedagogy requires both objective and subjective evidences. Even more so, my classroom lives confirm Dunne's description of praxis: a pursuit of excellence and an appreciation of classroom communities 'as constitutive of a worthwhile way of life'. Classroom lives as a series of communal activities not confined to rules, procedures, outcomes but rather transformation, self-realisation. And as this is an intimate process it entails self-revelation ... and so ...

Notes

1 According to *TES* this has since increased as 'In the eight years since the launch of the Education Endowment Fund, half of England's schools (more than 12,000) have now taken part in an EEF study' (Ward, 2019a).
2 Regarding marking, a main finding of Elliott et al. (2016) is that 'The quality of existing evidence focused specifically on written marking is low.'
3 NFER has offices in Swansea and York.

References

Aristotle. 2018. *Metaphysics*. Translated by W. D. Ross. Available from: http://classics.mit.edu/Aristotle/metaphysics.mb.txt [Accessed 1 September 2019]

BERA. 2014. *Research and the teaching profession: building the capacity for a self-improving education system*. London: BERA.

Carr, W. 1986. Theories of theory and practice. *Journal of Philosophy of Education* 20(2) 177-186.

Cartwright, N. 2019. What is meant by 'rigour' in evidence-based educational policy and what's so good about it? *Educational Research and Evaluation: An International Journal on Theory and Practice* 25(1-2) 63-80. Special issue. The Evidential Basis of 'Evidence-Based Education'.

Cowen, N. 2019. For whom does 'what works' work? The political economy of evidence-based education. *Educational Research and Evaluation: An International Journal on Theory and Practice* 25(1-2) 81-98. Special issue. The Evidential Basis of 'Evidence-Based Education'.

Dunne, J. 1997. *Back to the Rough Ground: Practical Judgement and the Lure of Technique*. Notre Dame, IN: University of Notre Dame Press.

EEF (Education Endowment Foundation). 2018. [Online] *Annual report 2018*. Available from: https://educationendowmentfoundation.org.uk/public/files/Annual_Reports/EEF_-_2018_Annual_Report_print.pdf [Accessed 4 September 2019]

Elliott, V., Baird, J.-A., Hopfenbeck, T. N., Ingram, J., Thompson, I., Usher, N., Zantout, M., Richardson, J. and Coleman, R. 2016. [Online] *A marked improvement? A review of the evidence on written marking*. Oxford University/Education Endowment Foundation. Available from: https://educationendowmentfoundation.org.uk/public/files/Presentations/Publications/EEF_Marking_Review_April_2016.pdf [Accessed 7 September 2019]

Joyce, K. E. 2019. The key role of representativeness in evidence-based education. *Educational Research and Evaluation: An International Journal on Theory and Practice* 25(1-2) 43-62. Special issue. The Evidential Basis of 'Evidence-Based Education'.

Kvernbekk, T. 2019. Practitioner tales: possible roles for research evidence in practice. *Educational Research and Evaluation: An International Journal on Theory and Practice* 25(1-2) 25-42. Special issue. The Evidential Basis of 'Evidence-Based Education'.

Lampl, P. 2011. [Online] Here's our chance to find out what works in addressing the shameful attainment gap between rich and poor. *Times Education Supplement*. 11 July 2011. Available from: www.tes.com/news/heres-our-chance-find-out-what-works-addressing-shameful-attainment-gap-between-rich-and-poor [Accessed 4 September 2019]

Nevill, C. 2016. [Online] *EEF Blog: Do EEF trials meet the new 'gold standard'?* 5 April 2016. Available from: https://educationendowmentfoundation.org.uk/news/do-eef-trials-meet-the-new-gold-standard/ [Accessed 12 September 2019]

Nutt, J. 2018. [Online] Research schools are stuck in a quagmire. *Times Education Supplement*. 30 June 2018. Available from: www.tes.com/news/research-schools-are-stuck-quagmire [Accessed 11 July 2019]

Phillips, D. C. 2019. Evidence of confusion about evidence of causes: comments on the debate about EBP in education. *Educational Research and Evaluation: An International Journal on Theory and Practice* 25(1-2) 7-14. Special issue. The Evidential Basis of 'Evidence-Based Education'.

Simpson, A. 2019a. Editorial. The evidential basis of 'evidence-based education': an introduction to the special issue. *Educational Research and Evaluation: An International Journal on Theory and Practice* 25(1-2) 1-6. Special issue. The Evidential Basis of 'Evidence-Based Education'.

Simpson, A. 2019b. Separating arguments from conclusions: the mistaken role of effect size in educational policy research. *Educational Research and Evaluation: An International Journal on Theory and Practice* 25(1-2) 99-109. Special issue. The Evidential Basis of 'Evidence-Based Education'.

Stenhouse, L. 1980a. [Online] Product or process? A reply to Brian Crittenden. *New Education* 2(1) 137-140. Available from: www.uea.ac.uk/documents/4059364/4994243/Stenhouse-1980-Product+or+Process-A+Reply+to+Brian+Crittenden.pdf/466fbb18-2037-4e83-8e99-9cc184e551e8 [Accessed 13 September 2019]

Stenhouse, L. 1980b. [Online] *What counts as research?* Draft paper. Centre for Applied Research in Education, University of East Anglia. December 1980. Available from: www.uea.ac.uk/documents/4059364/4994243/Stenhouse-1980-What+counts+as+research.pdf/416a405d-4e84-46a0-b4d9-cbd31815ade7 [Accessed 27 August 2019]

The Economist. 2018. [Online] The big classroom experiment: England has become one of the world's biggest education laboratories. *The Economist*. 31 March 2018. Available from: www.economist.com/britain/2018/03/31/england-has-become-one-of-the-worlds-biggest-education-laboratories [Accessed 4 September 2019]

Ward, H. 2019a. [Online] Research Schools Network expands to boost teaching. *Times Educational Supplement*. 11 July 2019. Available from: www.tes.com/news/research-schools-network-expands-boost-teaching [Accessed 9 September 2019]

Ward, H. 2019b. [Online] Meet Sir Kevan Collins – champion of education research. *Times Educational Supplement*. 13 September 2019. Available from: www.tes.com/news/meet-sir-kevan-collins-champion-education-research [Accessed 14 September 2019]

Wiliam, D. 2019. [Online] Some reflections on the role of evidence in improving education. *Educational Research and Evaluation: An International Journal on Theory and Practice* 25(1-2) 127-139. Special issue. The Evidential Basis of 'Evidence-Based Education'. Available from: www.tandfonline.com/doi/full/10.1080/13803611.2019.1617993?scroll=top&needAccess=true [Accessed 12 September 2019]

Wrigley, T. and McCusker, S. 2019. Evidence-based teaching: a simple view of 'science'. *Educational Research and Evaluation: An International Journal on Theory and Practice* 25(1-2) 110-126. Special issue. The Evidential Basis of 'Evidence-Based Education'.

8 A journey of praxis

It's in their eyes Tony, you can see it in their eyes!

These words are from the lips of John Weierter, assistant head teacher, as he strides into the cramped, open-plan area that I like to call 'my classroom'. And, with most teachers, this is where one's experience of evidence-based practices normally begins – the classroom. What do you see and hear in the classroom? Are the pupils noisy, quiet, busy, bored? Are they engaged with dialogue, workbooks, computers or switched off? There are myriad student responses – how do I know that I am helping them to make progress? And evidence, some evidence, is useful.

The self-revelation within this chapter is offered modestly. It is but one teacher's story – and everyone has a story to tell – perhaps, this story may resonate with some colleagues. The starting point, though, is somewhat surreal.

Oxford Street, Glasgow, Strathclyde Police Training Centre, 1976

I have a charge to prefer against you. You are not obliged to say anything in answer to the charge; but anything you do say will be taken down in writing and may be used against you. Surname?
McCann.
First name?
Genghis.

An outbreak of loud guffaws from the callow recruits. The training sergeant is experienced, masterly – he knows this will break the tension. And he also knows that we will remember this lesson. And 44 years later, he's proven to be right.

So, my formative experiences with *evidence* began before the classroom in the mid to late 1970s; and this concern for evidence even features within classroom curricula such as:

the Year 11 Making Moral decisions course in which I introduced real-life case studies. The Alexandria Axe-Man, Bonhill Bungle, Cathkin Capers and Dalmarnock Dilemma. True stories of a revenge-seeking brother-in-law; a police slip-up enabling a cheeky burglary; a snake-like but rapid police car chase from the centre of Scotland's biggest city to the edge of Europe's largest housing estate; and a cowering of policemen as the barrel of a rifle emerges from a window shutter.

(Luby 2019: 41)

However, a classroom-based concern for evidence really began in the late 1980s when, after a couple of years in post at Earlston High School in the Scottish Borders, I became immersed with the Borders Enterprise Initiative. This initiative introduced me to *enterprise learning* and *evidence-based classroom practices*. Reflecting upon a long career in the classroom, this is the one initiative in which the stars aligned. Reflective, evidence-based classroom practices supported the aims of local government that, in turn, were in accord with government policy. Unusual, isn't it? That it is unusual is alleged by Alex Moore (2012) with his contention that there is often a serious mismatch between teachers' perceptions of the purposes of education and those of government.

The late 1980s though? Relevant for today's classrooms? You may well ask. However, I side with Richard Evans (2011) when he asserts with respect to the Technical and Vocational Education Initiative (TVEI) that 'In many ways much of the success and examples of good practice remain localized, but I would argue that these elements *still merit further analysis and evaluation* [emphasis added].'

Enterprise

The second Thatcher-led UK Government had instituted TVEI under the agency of the Manpower Services Commission (MSC). Local education authorities were expected to institute different methods of delivering, managing, organising and resourcing programmes of technical and vocational education. Among its stated aims, it was anticipated that TVEI would:

- widen and enrich the curriculum;
- prepare students for the world of work; and
- help students to 'learn how to learn' (Evans 2011).

In order to achieve this, local authorities were granted a fair degree of autonomy as to how they implemented TVEI aims and the funding for this scheme was relatively generous. The Scottish Borders incarnation of TVEI was termed *enterprise learning* and driven forward by a triumvirate.

Triumvirate

This triumvirate comprised a *practical academic*, a *reflective practitioner* and a *practical visionary*. Appointed by TVEI/MSC to be the internal evaluator for the Borders Enterprise Initiative, the *practical academic* was Douglas Weir; then Director of Research at Jordanhill College of Education, Glasgow.[1] Through coordinating the national pilot Standard Grade course Social and Vocational Skills, Douglas had gained valuable experience of working with teachers who had been encouraged to reflect upon and share their teaching experiences.

The second member of the triumvirate and a prime example of a *reflective practitioner* was Martin Marroni, then principal teacher of English at Hawick High School. Already known for his innovative teaching, Martin was approached by the Borders TVEI Pilot Project Director and from their meeting ensued:

> a broad agreement that the aims of TVEI and the English department at Hawick High had much in common ... In Marroni's estimation ... 'they (TVEI) were looking to develop initiative in pupils, for pupils to be given more responsibility, and they were looking for development really of teaching strategies that would enhance, that would reflect what TVEI wanted'.
>
> (Luby 1995:22)

The *practical visionary* was Kate Houston. Through her work with mini-companies at the Borders TVEI centre; positive feedback from both Stirling and Glasgow conferences about such work; and organising TVEI dramatic productions, Kate was becoming convinced that lessons gleaned from 'enterprise mini-companies' could be applied to her subject area of English and, indeed, across the curriculum. In 1986, Kate took on part-time teaching duties at Hawick High School and this entailed team teaching three periods per week with Martin Marroni. Kate found that, to a large extent, her work had already been accomplished regarding enterprise learning as 'on arriving at Hawick ... Martin (Marroni) had fully thought out and developed this approach in his subject' (Luby, 1995:23). Kate Houston became the regional lynchpin of enterprise learning as in a new, expanded role as an assistant adviser, she helped to roll out Martin's fully developed pedagogy across the nine Scottish Borders' secondary schools.

T L hooked

In the spring term of 1988, I was blissfully unaware of what was about to transpire. My knowledge of 'Enterprise' was limited to the fictional *Star Trek* spaceship: but all of this was about to '*boldly go*'. The other eight Borders' secondary schools had participated with Enterprise in-service activities and programmes; but our head teacher had resisted. There seemed to be no need. Indeed, there was suspicion given its strong links with the increasingly unpopular Thatcher Government. TVEI and Enterprise seemed tainted; but 'resistance was futile' as the regional authority decreed that Earlston High School must participate with Kate Houston's regional in-service day. And so, reluctantly, we did.

Crossed arms and baleful looks are the unwelcoming signals from the scowl of teachers that await Kate Houston. Enterprise learning will be no 'easy sell' at Earlston. But, we are quickly disarmed. Referencing the not too distant turn of the millennium, Kate asks what kind of attributes should we be producing in our learners? A hand crawls upwards and a solitary voice mumbles 'Flexible'. Dutifully, Kate writes this up on the whiteboard. 'Em, adaptable' squeaks a second voice and, again, this is written up. The pace quickens. 'Inventive' growls another: added to the list. Confidence grows. The list grows. We are now offering 'creativity' and 'imagination' amongst others. The list is impressive. We think so anyway.

And then, my world turns upside down. Glancing at the whiteboard, then fixing us with a look, Kate enquires, 'Are *your* learners like this? Adaptable, creative, flexible, imaginative, inventive.' 'What!?' we splutter; we thought she was looking for good ideas – for other people. Does she seriously think our classrooms are like this? Priding ourselves on our levels of academic attainment, our classrooms are serried, ranked, obedient. However, throughout the day, Kate engages us with different ways to think about our classrooms, our rows, our students, our expectations. We participate with problem-solving exercises, role play activities; we teach and learn from peers. Her in-service day is active, engaging and, in my case, it is inspiring.

The dawning cold light

Come the following morning, though? Yes, yesterday was inspiring, surprisingly so: but was not that due to the contrived environment of an in-service day? This enterprise learning couldn't really work in my classroom; could it? But there was more. The final element of this level 1 in-service day requires homework i.e. for us to engage with an enterprise-based lesson with our own students (see Figure 8.1).

That homework lesson is lost in the mists of time; but it must have been encouraging as I signed up for level 2 (see Figure 8.2).

Again, I recall little of the event but it was sufficiently motivating that, along with a teacher of home economics and a teacher of biology, I signed up for the third level, six-week course as given in Figure 8.3.

Today, much is made of the value of *lesson study* (e.g. Dudley, 2015) and rightly so. But education is a sieve. According to the Teacher Development Trust, lesson study entails:

---

1. After being introduced to the aims of the enterprising approach, usually through a brainstorming session, course members participate in problem-solving exercises.
2. In groups, course members teach each other by methods which are deemed to be enterprising.
3. Participants give each other feedback about the above activities.
4. In the final session, participants prepare a lesson, in their own subject area, taking account of the aims and methods with which they have been involved throughout the day.

Figure 8.1 Enterprise Level 1 programme
Source: Luby (1995: 24)

Session 1
A half-day meeting approximately 10 days prior to session 2. With the school coordinator, the course participants settle administrative details, such as teaching groups, classes to be used, joint preparation of lessons.

Session 2
One day, in the morning, each participant takes it in turn to teach a class and to observe fellow group members doing likewise.
In the afternoon, there is feedback on and analysis of the morning's teaching episodes.

Figure 8.2 Enterprise Level 2 programme
Source: Luby (1995: 24)

Stage 1
Half-day meeting of three teachers to prepare for this six-week course. Each member of this cross-
   curricular group would take responsibility for one of the following areas:
      (a) Role of the individual pupil in group work;
      (b) Implications of this enterprising approach for syllabus construction;
      (c) Requirements for classroom management with this approach.

Stage 2
Each teacher identifies a class for this course. There is a requirement to 'team-teach' with each
   other for two periods a week. Thus the group focuses on three different classes with each
   teacher having a team teaching commitment of four periods a week. There is one further period
   a week set aside for the group to evaluate and plan.

Stage 3
Half-day meeting for evaluation and consideration of further implementation of the enterprising
   approach.

Figure 8.3 Enterprise Level 3 programme
Source: Luby (1995: 24)

teacher-led research in which a triad of teachers work together to target an identified
area for development in their students' learning. Using existing evidence, participants
collaboratively research, plan, teach and observe a series of lessons, using ongoing discussion, reflection and expert input to track and refine their interventions.

(https://tdtrust.org/what-is-lesson-study)

This serves well as a summative description of the Enterprise programme that took place
decades prior. Indeed, as Moore (2012: 170) points out in his tribute to the curriculum giant,
Vic Kelly, 'arguments ... that were being engaged with nearly thirty-five years ago are still so
relevant today'. And now, more than 30 years later, I contend likewise that we can still learn
from the TVEI experience of enterprise learning.

Foundational

Undoubtedly, the Borders Enterprise Initiative was *the most influential experience of my
career*. Working in a cross-curricular cell of three teachers; observing fellow teachers; analysing, discussing and sharing lesson plans; reviewing our own lessons and those of others –
all of this *built trust*. The triad taught the same pupils and, as with all teachers, each of us
desired that our pupils' learning be enhanced: however, a cautionary note. According to the
EEF evaluation information of 181 schools with 12,700 pupils in Years 4 and 5 taking part in
an efficacy trial for lesson study between February 2015 and November 2017 – lesson study
does not work. When EEF looked at attainment outcomes for pupils at the end of Year 6, they
'found no evidence of impact in this well-run, high-security trial.'[2]

However, these lesson studies were not focusing on enterprise learning; because the
Scottish Borders' TVEI version of enterprise learning did have *impact*. So, what exactly was
enterprise learning?

Borders Enterprise

Enterprise learning began in the early 1980s with Martin Marroni experimenting with innovative pedagogy at Jedburgh Grammar School. He would invite colleagues into his classroom to review and comment upon different pedagogic practices. He asked the students for their views: and it didn't work. Martin admits himself that he was too rushed, too enthusiastic; and failed to take his colleagues with him. Lessons were learned. Upon moving to the larger Hawick High School, Martin slowed down with his innovation: but he still innovated. He still invited colleagues into his classes. He still sought comments from students. But at a slower pace: and this worked.

Martin's inventive approach to developing pedagogy caught the eye of a rugby giant: Jim Telfer. The very same Jim Telfer who had also learned a harsh lesson: as head coach of the British Lions he suffered a whitewash (0-4) at the hands of the All Blacks. But he was resilient and learning from this experience, as head coach, he led Scotland to the Grand Slam in the 1984 Rugby Five Nations tournament. Likewise, within the world of education. Following the example of his head teacher mentor at Deans Community High School in the Central Belt new town of Livingston; he exercised patience. Whilst Halwick head teacher Telfer was seeking out innovation, Martin walked through the front door. His classroom practices, his relationships with colleagues and students were *different*.

Jim Telfer's support for Martin's approach caused division amongst the staff. However, just as the All Blacks were masters of their craft, so too Martin was a master of pedagogy. Both sought continuous improvement: as did Telfer. And the fruits of Martin's reflective practice? See Figure 8.4.

As Martin says himself, 'I have been able to build my theories on what I have done in practice, as are seen in the Enterprise documents; it's my ordering, it reflects therefore my philosophy of teaching' (interview, 7 February 1990). His claim is confirmed by the other two triumvirate members who acknowledge that pupils should be given more responsibility for their learning, and that this can be achieved through 'lessons (which) have to be carefully structured ... built on purposeful interaction ... to extend the range of activities in which pupils participate' (Weir and Houston, 1988).

Again, it is worth noting that this form of enterprise learning was ahead of its time and that it is relevant for today's classrooms. In a June 2019 edition of the *Times Education Supplement*, Geoff Leask, the chief executive of Young Enterprise Scotland, bewails the lack of recognition afforded to enterprise education. In so doing, he seems oblivious to the work of Kate Houston and enterprise mini-companies in the mid-1980s – again we confront Moore's span of 35 years – a generation of forgetfulness. And recall that the Borders form of enterprise learning was not a separate activity from routine classroom practices; it was embedded within this routine. It was *how* teachers taught and *how* students learned – the three elements of structure, interaction and activity.

Praxis – first major step

By the late 1980s this Borders TVEI programme of enterprise learning engaged a large number of teachers with innovative teaching and reflective practice. However, at the time,

---

STRUCTURE

The structure of the activity is clearly presented to the pupils, so that they understand the goal or outcome and the steps involved in achieving it.

The structure gives clear guidelines while at the same time it allows opportunity for pupils to use their initiative.

In group activities each pupil has a clearly identified responsibility. There is a mutually agreed time-scale for the activity which takes account of the amount of work required for successful completion.

INTERACTION

The activity gives the opportunity for co-operation and for the exercise of individual responsibility.

Pupils are given the opportunity to work outside the direct supervision of the teacher.

There is an element of real choice in the activity and each pupil has the right to opt out.

There is a creative approach to dealing with disruption.

The conditions for teacher intervention are clearly understood by the pupils.

There is the opportunity for feedback, from pupil to teacher, from teacher to pupil, and from pupil to pupil.

ACTIVITIES

Pupils work towards PRESENTING something to another group.

Pupils work towards SOLVING a problem.

Pupils are involved in ASSESSING their own work or the work of others.

Pupils work towards TEACHING other pupils what they have learned.

Pupils are involved in CREATING an artefact.

Pupils are involved in ORGANISING an activity.

Figure 8.4 The three elements of enterprising teaching and learning
Source: SBC (1989: 22)

'discussion with colleagues ... consistently reveals ... there is no doubt that the pupils are enthusiastic and motivated *but* there is a genuine concern that it is too time consuming and that the syllabus *cannot be fully covered*' (Luby, 1990: 13, emphases added). This intrigued and challenged me. But what to do about it? Well, according to Moore (2012: 36):

> Teachers should perceive themselves as researchers and theorists as well as practitioners. *Action research* is a particularly valuable way for teachers to evaluate and critique their own current practice and to move in an informed and principled way towards more effective future practice.

And this was the first major step in the journey of *praxis*. No longer a teacher – now becoming a teacher-as-researcher. I wished to obtain more detailed research evidence about enterprising classroom practices: but none was readily available. I recalled the final year of my Bachelor of Education degree with Strathclyde University – saturated with psychology. I still had my notes in a folder – somewhere – and after rustling around, I found them. *Quasi-experiment*. Now, wouldn't that be interesting? I could teach some of my classes by the traditional, didactic, teacher-centred approach. Yes, make it interesting – quizzes, good video clips, etc. – do my best for the children. *A control group*. Other classes could be taught by this new, active, enterprising approach. Again, do my best for the children. *An experimental group*.

So, armed with a folder full of notes, I took my first steps as a teacher-researcher by committing to conduct a quasi-experiment with four classes of seventy-seven S1 (Y8) pupils. Thirty-seven of whom were to be taught by an *academic approach*, whilst the remaining forty were taught by an *enterprising approach*.

Academic approach – the learning situation was passive. The pupils were confined to the classroom area with movement being centred round the teacher's desk as pupils came out to ask for help. All pupil work was marked by the teacher with a system of 'credits' as a means of extrinsic motivation. The teacher's role could be summarised as regularly marking work, explaining from the blackboard or a book, helping when difficulties arose and updating pupil credit sheets.

Enterprising approach – the learning situation was active. The pupils were free to move around the classroom and often used nearby working areas and two other areas well removed from the classroom (with infrequent supervision). The pupils were required to make two group presentations in forms of their own choosing e.g. song, model, play, quiz show, etc. The teacher's role was to move round groups, offering suggestions, constructively criticising and assessing presentations (Luby, 2007:17–18).

Determined to be *rigorous*, I contacted the Scottish Council for Research in Education (SCRE) for advice. Marion Devine at the Schools Assessment and Research Unit at SCRE advised me that for reliability the test items should be matched with learning objectives; and so for the pre-test there were four test items for each of the four learning objectives; and this increased to twenty test items for each of the four learning objectives in both the end-unit test and the re-test. Additionally, acting upon guidance from Pamela Munn at SCRE, the pupils' pre-test determined their placement into one of seven ability ranges based on their performance in four skills. Prior to this work on Hinduism (December 1988 to May 1989) colleagues in teaching and the advisory service, working individually, matched up a random order of learning objectives with test questions. From this exercise a consensus on learning objectives – test items became apparent.

Learning objectives – the four skills tested were based on Barrett's taxonomy of the lower order skills: (a) literal comprehension and (b) re-organisation; and the higher order skills of (c) inferential comprehension and (d) evaluation (Luby, 2007).

Having been taught the same Hinduism content – over the same length of time – by the two different approaches; the pupils were then tested for their short-term performance. My interim conclusion (Luby, 1989) was that whilst an academic approach may be more appropriate for the pupils with higher test results; the enterprising approach favoured the pupils experiencing more difficulty with their learning. However, if the affective domain of learning were to be taken into consideration, then the majority of pupils preferred the enterprising approach. Statistically, though, the differences were not significant.

Six months later I re-tested the pupils and the results, this time, were *statistically significant*. The more highly ranked academic pupils performed better if they had participated with the Hinduism content through an enterprising approach; and the lower ranked pupils also retained information better through the medium of enterprise learning than through a didactic approach. In both cases the students had invested more of their own ideas, more of themselves, into their classwork.

This was also exemplified in other areas of the RE curriculum. For example, one group humorously, but not irreverently, adapted Monty Python's *Life of Brian* movie into a presentation on Christianity.[3] Another group teaching about the eight-fold path in Buddhism were inspired by Robert Kirkwood's (1988) brilliantly illustrated cartoon book *Looking for Happiness*. Using role play, they visually presented the eight-fold path as a bus journey comprising eight stops *en route* to the terminus of *nirvana*. The bus stops represented right views, intention, speech, action, livelihood, effort, mindfulness and concentration; and passengers alighted from the bus at the appropriate stop e.g. a passenger found to be a butcher had to leave at bus stop no. 5. This apparently deeper and more meaningful approach to learning was corroborated through unsolicited comments from the pupils themselves e.g. after performing a 'rap' about Hindu gods one pupil exclaimed 'I'll remember that for the rest of my life!' (Luby, 1989: 9).

From the perspective of Alex Moore above, I was becoming a teacher-researcher and I concluded that:

> an enterprising approach to the teaching/learning situation does not inhibit academic performance (and) when pupils are trusted and encouraged to be creative they respond favourably. The classroom atmosphere is 'busy and productive', the learning which takes place is meaningful and longer lasting.

> (Luby 1990: 13)

From the perspective of *technical reason*, this quasi-experiment had focused on learning outcomes and there was sufficient data, ample objective evidence, to demonstrate the success of this enterprising approach to learning and teaching in my classroom teaching of religious education. But there was a niggle. What about subjective evidence? None of this had been collated yet alone analysed and quantified. Sure, there were informal, supportive comments from staff and pupils: but quantifiable evidence? None.

Praxis – second major step

This lack of subjective evidence triggered the second major step of *praxis*. Moore (2012) suggests that a teacher should theorise about educational practices and this began, for me, in the staffroom. A colleague, Don Ledingham,[4] returned from a three-year second-ment at then Moray House College of Education in Edinburgh.[5] Don was aware of my 'curiosity' regarding educational practices and, at a morning break, he handed me an academic paper suggesting that I may wish to have a look at it. And I did, reluctantly: but it was transformative.

Initially, I was reluctant as I had not read an academic paper for several years and, to compound matters, it was from the *Journal of Philosophy of Education*. Titled 'Theories of theory and practice' and written by Wilfred Carr, I had to 'shift up a gear or two' intellectually to come to terms with it; but it was well worth the effort. This paper has informed and underpinned much of my classroom practices and academic writings ever since. In his 1986 paper, Carr discusses approaches to educational practice and the first of these, *empiricist*, was of direct interest to me at that time.

At the outset, I perceived of the Borders Enterprise Initiative in *empiricist* terms. With regard to the form of knowledge of educational practice, Martin Marroni had drawn a general conclusion of three underpinning pedagogic principles from enterprise learning (SBC, 1989) namely, *structure, interaction* and *activity*. The observed facts were the numerous activities within his classroom and the subsequent experiments were conducted by many other teachers throughout the Borders region in their classrooms. The nature of classroom life was held to be instrumental as we were trying to develop the range of skills acquired by the pupils e.g. creativity, imagination, responsibility, etc. The in-service programme of Borders Enterprise levels 1-3 held our function to be technical in that we were applying the pedagogic principles of structure, interaction and activity in order to develop these aforementioned skills.

The interpretative approach to educational practice, though, had little been considered – and theorising through scholarship was the next step in this process of praxis. And so, I was encouraged by Douglas Weir to undertake a Master of Philosophy higher research degree.

Scholarship

I wanted to move from the objective evidence of test scores, raw data, to the more subjective evidence of what the pupils perceived and thought. From a survey of 287 pupils I was able to ascertain that in the estimation of the pupils 'an enterprising approach to teaching is distinctive from other teaching approaches ... (as) it is more likely to give them a structured learning environment in which they have opportunities to interact and to participate actively in the learning process' (Luby, 1993: 167) These findings from the pupils confirmed my own impressions and those of some colleagues.

I probed further and determined to ascertain which particular strategies were creating and sustaining a positive climate for learning and enabling the pupils to make progress with their learning. Again, in the estimation of the 287 pupils surveyed, they affirmed that the following eight strategies were consistent and significant:

1. working towards teaching other pupils what they have learned;
2. often being involved in creating things e.g. model, play;
3= having a real choice in the work to be done;
3= working towards presenting something to another group or the class;
3= being involved in assessing their own work or the work of others;
6. often having the opportunity to get feedback from other pupils;
7. often being given the opportunity to work outside the direct supervision of the teacher; and
8. often being involved in organising things to do.

(Luby 1993:169)

In my estimation, the classroom was becoming less a collection of individuals – who were ranked competitively; rather, it was becoming more a community of individuals – who collaborated. Through *group-based peer teaching*, each and every individual pupil had a responsibility for each and every other pupil in the class. The teacher was *primus inter pares* in the classroom; but the sum of all of the pupils' talents, skills and abilities far outweighs those of the classroom teacher. Those with artistic abilities draw posters and wrought art-work for the attention and benefit of their fellow pupils; whilst those with musical abilities sing and rap for their peers. They evaluate each other's work through the group teaching presentations:

- Content: how much new information do we learn?
- Interest: how interesting – or not – is the presentation?
- Organisation: clearly rehearsed or thrown together at the last minute?

They also assess the contribution of each of their group members and this peer assessment galvanises the few pupils who, at the outset, tried to rely on the contributions from others to overcome their lack of input. All of this contributed to rendering radically different the atmos-phere, format and ethos of the classroom.

In tandem with these changes, I now began to *theorise* about educational practices (Moore, 2012) – moving the focus from within the classroom and outwards. An indication of such theorising was the dissertation being titled *Democracy and the classroom: lessons from the Borders Enterprise Initiative*. This better represented the democratic nature of the classroom.

However, a fundamental personal and professional transformation was also taking place – something more than becoming a teacher-researcher-theorist. The renowned Australian edu-cationist, Judyth Sachs, has a good description of this transformation.

Transformation through activist teacher professionalism

Activist teacher professionalism is essentially about a politics of transformation. Its spheres of interest are concerned with changing people's beliefs, perspectives and opinions about the importance of teaching ... The politics of transformation are rooted in everyday life and this is its strength.

(Sachs 2003:12)

So declares Judyth Sachs in her plenary address to the British Educational Research Association Conference at Edinburgh when discussing her ground-breaking work with regard to 'activist teaching professionalism'. For Sachs, an activist teacher professional is *not* the governmental concept of 'the modern professional ... (being) one who works efficiently and effectively in meeting standardised criteria' (Whitty, 2006). Rather, it should be concerned with 'the formation of human beings who think critically, act ethically and seek justice throughout their lives' (Mockler and Normanhurst, 2004).

Sachs's concept of the activist teaching professional clearly influenced the General Teaching Council Scotland as they thought through the introduction of the Chartered Teacher Scheme within Scottish education. In The Standard for Chartered Teacher, the GTCS (2009) assert that:

Chartered Teachers are expected to be at the forefront of critically engaging with practice and to take a leading role in its development and implementation of change in current and future educational initiatives ... The Chartered Teacher embraces and actively promotes the values, principles and practices of equality and social justice.

This was a new role for teachers. However, as outlined in the opening pages of this book, despite a launch with much fanfare and goodwill, its demise was both swift and unwelcome. Nonetheless, it is this kind of type of teacher whom we need to commit to working in areas of deprivation in order to close the attainment gap. Thankfully, there are hopeful signs south of the Tweed. Albeit in a different form, the Chartered College of Teaching has revived the status of Chartered Teacher. The attainment of such is highly demanding (https://chartered. college/chartered-teacher) and requires participants 'to showcase their knowledge and skills against the areas set out in the Chartered College's Professional Principles' (https:// chartered.college/chartered-teacher/professional-principles).

On Tuesday, 14 May 2019, I had the opportunity and privilege to undertake a profes- sional conversation with Sophie Longney who was soon to graduate in the first cohort of Chartered Teachers. This took place at her school, The Sir Donald Bailey Academy, Newark, Nottinghamshire. Borrowing from Mockler and Normanhurst (2004) above – 'Was I in the company of a teacher who thinks critically, acts ethically and seeks justice?'

Thinking critically

AL: So, Sophie, could you tell me please about the school-based research project that you did for your Chartered Teacher award?

SOPHIE: Okay, so I'm English Lead for Sir Donald Bailey and also Head of Teaching and Learning; and for the past few years end of Key Stage 2 results have shown that reading, comprehension is our sort of weakest area across school. So, obviously, one of our pri- orities to improve. So, started doing a bit of research into how we teach reading compre- hension specifically within Key Stage 2 and at this point we were doing guided reading carousels. So, traditional guided reading – the children are in ability groups and each group is reading a different book to suit their ability. The teacher works with one group each day; so say you've got four days you would get around each group. The rest of the days, the children would be working independently on either a pre-task or a post-task from their guided reading session with the teacher.

Now, when I started delving into research about the process of guided reading carousels and how effective they are; the research came back saying that 'Yes, the time that you spend with each group is very, very valuable because you're working with a small group of pupils, maybe 4–5 children each day and they get a really rich experience.' However, what is the quality of what the independent groups are doing? Because, for it to work effectively you do have to really give that group all of your attention; and if the independent groups weren't working as effectively as that guided group – it did then mean that the children really only get one quality teacher led session from the expert in the room once a week.

... So looked into all of that, a lot of research was moving to a whole class teaching approach ... and our children were struggling. So, we went down the route of whole class teaching instead – rather than guided group work – and we've noticed a massive improvement. So, it targets all children on a daily basis, all children benefit from having the expert leading the session. Same sort of thing, we do a lot of scaffolding, input the objective, model how to do the task and then all the children apply it independently. You also still get the time to work with a guided group during each session. You still can mix it up a little bit; but it means all children get the input each day and all children are explicitly taught the skills that they need to succeed in reading comprehension.

AL: How do you know this works? What's your evidence that this change of approach –

SOPHIE: Classroom-based evidence, so –

AL: Like what?

SOPHIE: And results, so we ... obviously monitor the children's progress on a regular basis and I can see that since we've implemented this new way of teaching, results have benefitted and the children are more confident asking the different types of questions because they've had it modelled on a more regular basis.

[...]

AL: And you had a mentor for the *CTeach* programme?

SOPHIE: I did, yes.

AL: So you must have spoken with him or her about your project?

SOPHIE: Yeah, I did; and we also had at one point an expert interview. So, it was a phone call with a professional who ... I had a literature review and she challenged me on it really; and that was really useful because it got me thinking about other sorts of areas to consider. She was sort of arguing that that quality of the guided group, that you got with the guided reading carousel shouldn't be lost. So that is why I went from whole class teaching to then starting to experiment with working with ... once they've had their input and they've had it modelled, still working with a specific group of children each day to sort of blend the approaches a bit.

As well through Chartered Teacher we did video portfolios – so videoing my own practice, that was really useful because again I linked it in – and I videoed some of my own reading sessions. That was useful because I was able to reflect on a range of things. Children's attention, their concentration throughout the lesson, as well as then being able to look at obviously their work at the end and ultimately their results.

There can be little doubt that I am in the presence of a teacher who *thinks critically*. Sophie critiques a group-based form of 'carousel reading' prevailing within her school and she moves to an approach based on whole class teaching. However, heeding the advice of her *CTeach* mentor, Sophie retains a strength of group learning and, ultimately, blends both approaches together. Notably, the *CTeach* programme had a significant role to play through a review of the literature, an interview with an expert and the use of video portfolios.

Acting ethically

AL: Did you ever give any thought to having like a randomised control trial and say, 'Right, we'll have half the staff doing the carousel approach and half of the staff doing the whole class approach'?

SOPHIE: Yeah, I did consider it, but then I knew from past experience that the ... we needed to change and for me it just seemed unfair to give some of our children an opportunity and not the rest. So ...

Another solution, of course, is to have the teachers and classes 'switch around' from being control groups (carousel) to experimental groups (whole class). Of further concern, though, and deriving from the 1975 classic work of Lawrence Stenhouse, *An Introduction to Curriculum Development and Research*, there is an ethical imperative for an '*extended professional*' having undertaken a rigorous investigation into classroom practices to then share these findings with interested others. Are there examples of this taking place across The Forge Trust?

AL: So, do you collaborate with other schools at all ... How does that work?

SOPHIE: ... Yeah, it's a very supportive collaboration with the other English leads that I have. So, yeah, they've all ... we all learn from each other, as well, because another teacher at one of our other schools has delved into vocabulary strand in a lot more detail – and from that she sort of implemented these vocabulary starters which, again, we've taken on board here as well. So it's ... working together really to improve results across the Trust. Yeah, we do see ourselves as a team really rather than isolated schools ...

AL: Is there anything you've taken on board from the other schools ...?

SOPHIE: Yeah, those vocabulary starters, yeah they came from Parkgate, so that was really good ... this is not to do with reading now but we have taken on some handwriting ... skills from Forest View within the Trust. One of those being handwriting lines in children's exercise books. We've sort of taken that on board this year after their recommendation really and, yeah, we've seen an improvement in children's handwriting too. So, now that's fully implemented across the Trust.

Clearly there is collaboration across The Forge Trust's schools through learning from and sharing with each other. So, there is evidence of *thinking critically* and *acting ethically* – what of *seeking justice*?

Seeking justice

SOPHIE: ... now I know we've got a rigorous method for teaching the skills and children having a good understanding of comprehension – my next sort of step is to improve their knowledge of the world really, to be able ... to allow them to access the texts even better. Because a lot of our children struggle with an understanding of vocabulary and language. So we're in quite a disadvantaged area of Nottinghamshire, I'm sure you're aware –

AL: Oh yes, uh huh.

SOPHIE: Of the surroundings, they come in behind where they should be expectation wise and it's a common trend really, they don't have a broad range of vocabulary and language skills. So my next step, really, to push this on even further; and I'll be doing this now I've become a Chartered Teacher, not necessarily for the project of some sort but ... really making sure even if they don't get those experiences in their own lives outside of school, make sure they get experiences within school; and that they've opened their eyes to lots of different cultures around the world from our lessons in school. So, hopefully, once I've then got the combination of both of those things, not only will they be able to answer the questions that go with a reading test and understand the comprehension element of it, they'll also when they look at these texts, they'll have just a better understanding of vocabulary and understanding of where these things come from and the different cultures.

[...]

AL: I want to just ask you; why did you choose to work in an area of deprivation ...?

SOPHIE: Yeah, well I've ... I love working here with the children in this area. I think I would argue that it's more rewarding because you see ... you see sort of where they've come from and then, when they go on to achieve great things, it gives you a lot of pride. Like this morning, they've done this reading test; I can see they've got confidence, they're coming out pleased with their achievements and that, for me, is ultimately what I came here for; and what I do all the research for as well: because it improves their life chances. And if we could just get a few of them going on to university in the future then it would be really, really amazing. I mean, a lot of parents can't read or write themselves – so for our children to achieve national expectations by the end of Year 6 it's ... really, really –

AL: It's a big thing.

SOPHIE: Yeah, rewarding; so that's what I enjoy about it the most I think.

AL: And how long have you been here?

SOPHIE: This is my fifth year.

Sophie's concern to seek justice for her children is readily apparent within her words. As the professional conversation moved towards the end Sophie spoke of her colleagues as:

> hardworking, ambitious, driven members of staff and obviously with that you do get teachers that are looking to improve their practice – and are keen and enthusiastic to do things outside of work: because your Masters is a commitment. Same with the Chartered Teacher.

Upon departing from Sophie and her school my feeling was of peace. A peace welling up from a recognition that as a retired, Chartered Teacher my journey of praxis was ending. However, the baton is passing to a new, younger generation of teachers who are embarking upon their journey of praxis – and already they demonstrate evidence of thinking critically, acting ethically and seeking justice.

Notes

1   Shortly thereafter, Europe's largest single provider of initial teacher education, Jordanhill College of Education, was subsumed within Strathclyde University.
2   Source: https://educationendowmentfoundation.org.uk/projects-and-evaluation/projects/lesson-study/
3   My main concern was that the British Board of Film Classification (BBFC) had classified the film with an AA certificate (no admission to persons under 14) and the children were too young to have watched it.
4   Don went on to have a stellar career becoming Director of Education at two local authorities – simultaneously!
5   Now Moray House School of Education, University of Edinburgh.

References

Carr, W. 1986. Theories of theory and practice. *Journal of Philosophy of Education* 20(2) 177–186.
Dudley, P. (Ed.) 2015. *Lesson Study: Professional Learning for Our Time*. Abingdon, Oxon: Routledge.
Evans, R. 2011. [Online] *The Technical and Vocational Education Initiative (TVEI) 1983–1997*. Available from: https://technicaleducationmatters.org/2011/11/12/the-technical-and-vocational-education-initiative-tvei-1983-1997/ [Accessed 2 July 2019]

GTCS (General Teaching Council Scotland). 2009. [Online] *The Standard for Chartered Teacher.* June 2009. Edinburgh: GTCS/The Scottish Government. Available from: https://dera.ioe.ac.uk/973/1/the-standard-for-chartered-teacher.pdf [Accessed 18 October 2019]

Kirkwood, R. 1988. *Looking for Happiness.* Harlow: Longman.

Leask, G. 2019. [Online] Why enterprise education must become a priority. *Times Education Supplement.* Available from: www.tes.com/news/why-enterprise-education-must-become-priority [Accessed 23 April 2020]

Luby, A. 1989. Teaching styles and pupil learning: interim report on research at Earlston High School. *Scottish Journal of Religious Education* 10(1) 6-9.

Luby, A. 1990. Teaching styles and pupil learning: concluding report on research at Earlston High School. *Scottish Journal of Religious Education* 10(3) 11-13.

Luby, A. 1993. *Democracy and the classroom: lessons from the Borders Enterprise Initiative.* Unpublished MPhil thesis. Glasgow: University of Strathclyde.

Luby, A. 1995. An enterprising approach to democratising the curriculum: reflections on a Scottish experience. *Journal of Vocational Education & Training* 47(1) 21-33.

Luby, A. 2007. Enterprise, academia, enlightenment: three acts in a professional's transformation. *Education Today: Journal of the College of Teachers* 57(3) 13-23.

Luby, A. 2019. The Holy Shroud and the classroom. *Shroud Newsletter* Issue 89(Summer): 40-43.

Mockler, N. and Normanhurst, L. 2004. *Transforming teachers: new professional learning and transformative teacher professionalism.* Paper presented to the Australian Association for Educational Research annual conference, University of Melbourne, 28 November to 2 December 2004.

Moore, A. 2012. *Teaching and Learning: Pedagogy, Curriculum and Culture.* 2nd ed. Abingdon, Oxon: Routledge.

Sachs, J. 2003. Teacher Activism: Mobilising the Profession. Plenary Address, British Educational Research Association Conference, Heriot-Watt University, Edinburgh, 11-13 September 2003.

SBC (Scottish Borders Council). 1989. *Enterprise Methods in Teaching and Learning.* Newtown St Boswells: Scottish Borders Council.

Stenhouse, L. 1975. *An Introduction to Curriculum Development and Research.* London: Heinemann.

Weir, D. and Houston, K. 1988. Why teachers must learn to think big. *The Times Educational Supplement.* 4 March 1988.

Whitty, G. 2006. *Teacher professionalism in a new era.* Paper presented at the first General Teaching Council for Northern Ireland Annual Lecture, Belfast, March 2006.

9 Strategic conversations
Backward and forward

Serendipity

During the writing of this book, I took up a new post with Northumbria University and one of the requirements for this post is subject lead for History – my favourite subject whilst both a school pupil and a university student. Indeed, it is the first subject that I taught whilst a student teacher in my first school placement at St Cuthbert's primary school in Burnbank – a Lanarkshire housing scheme renowned as the home of the late, great Jock Stein who managed both the 'Lisbon Lions' and the Scotland international football team.[1] Fittingly, given my previous occupation, it was the first in a series of lessons about the history of the police service. My biographical point is that expressed by James Baldwin (1924-1987) namely, 'Go back to where you started, or as far back as you can, examine all of it ... but *know whence you came* [emphasis added].'

As discussed earlier, education tends to have a sieve-like memory and we often find ourselves 're-inventing the wheel'. During the aforementioned enterprise learning initiative in the Scottish Borders, I was informed by a more experienced colleague, 'not to get too excited as it (enterprise learning) would return 15 years later wearing a different hat'. Sadly, his words proved to be prophetic. Exactly 15 years later, in the early noughties, I attended a 'Critical Skills training course' that, in all but name, was a re-enactment of enterprise learning. Ten days later, worse was to follow. A school twilight session on formative assessment posed similar questions and raised the same issues as had been discussed and analysed in the late 1980s, during meetings of our informal, Borders regional formative assessment group: even the hat was the same.

We need to know our history.

In Chapter 7, I recall Tom Bennet's humble, honest story of the birth of researchED. This organisation did not arise from nowhere; rather it sprang from a loamy soil. There is a rich history behind the current interest in research and evidence-based practices and Philippa Cordingley, Chief Executive of the Centre for the Use of Research and Evidence in Education (CUREE) is an excellent source of information and lived history. As the CUREE website details, Philippa is:

> an internationally acknowledged expert in using evidence to develop education policy and practice. She leads CUREE and has a hands on role in many of its projects including

... the creation of innovative practical resources to engage practitioners with research (e.g. Research for Teachers, The Research Informed Practice (TRIPs) web site and of a bank of micro-enquiry tools for the Economic and Social Research Council's Teaching and Learning Research Programme ...).

(www.curee.co.uk/about-us/staff-profiles/philippa-cordingley)

We join our professional conversation at the point of discussing the devastating Teacher Training Agency (TTA) annual lecture by David Hargreaves, then professor of education at the University of Cambridge. In this lecture Hargreaves delivers an astonishing *mea culpa* on behalf of the education research community. At the beginning of his second paragraph he confesses that:

The £50–60 million[2] we spend annually on educational research is poor value for money in terms of improving the quality of education provided in schools. In fundamental respects the teaching profession has, I believe, been inadequately served by us. It need not be so.

(Hargreaves 1996:1)

Hargreaves (1996: 3) continues by drawing an unflattering comparison between education and medicine and notes that with respect to the latter 'there is little difference between researchers and users: all are practitioners'. One can almost feel the knife twisting as he then comments:

Educational researchers write mainly for one another in their countless academic journals, which are not to be found in a school staffroom. It is this gap between researchers and practitioners which betrays the fatal flaw in educational research. For it is the researchers, not the practitioners, who determine the agenda of educational research.

(Hargreaves 1996:3)

Unsurprisingly, Hargreaves met with a storm of protest from his colleagues in the education research community but even they acknowledged the validity of some of his critique (e.g. Hammersley, 1997).[3] It certainly cast a dark cloud of suspicion over the worth of education research – and this had ramifications – as Philippa acknowledges below.

Wednesday, 26 June 2019
CUREE HQ, Coventry

PHILIPPA: ... Yes, and it was very controversial; it was an annual TTA lecture where he was rubbishing education research and –

AL: I remember that.

PHILIPPA: But just before he published that the research committee of the TTA which had people like Michael Barber and Caroline Cox, Antony O'Hare and David Hargreaves on it. We produced a policy about *promoting teaching as a research evidence-informed profession*, not based, informed; and developed three strands to that to establish a National Teacher Research Panel – to establish grants for teachers to do research [such] that ... it could be critiqued and published ... And to help schools build a culture where they were pulling through research in a self-conscious way as part of teachers' initial formation of

CPD. So we'd launched that before the Hargreaves ... *it sank without trace because of the controversy in the Hargreaves thing* [emphasis added].

[...]

and following in its footsteps was the Best Practice Research Scholarships. We set up the School Based Research Consortium; again, this is all on our website ... and at the same time I went to the National Union of Teachers and said 'We're going to have some top-down interesting stuff about this. In other countries professional associations are leading CPD. I know you're interested in CPD; you could be doing a bottom-up version of this.' So we set up –

AL: Again, what year are we talking about here?

PHILIPPA: 1998, I think, by then. So they set up ... enquiry-based co-coaching programmes between teachers working with leading researchers in the field over a year – which was an incredibly successful programme – and then they set up Teacher Research Grants too. So you've got bottom-up and top-down and then sideways-on; I started working with local authorities to encourage this. Though back ... in 1997 we did a survey of how many teachers said they had anything to do with research and it was either 3% or 4%. And most of them said they wouldn't let anyone know because they would think they were geeks; and in 2010 the GTCE's [General Teaching Council England] final census had some-thing ... I think something like over 40% of teachers saying either they were engaging with somebody else's research, either another teacher or an academic researcher, or engaging in their own research. So ... so, there was a big ... this was happening quietly over that decade between the late 1990s –

AL: That last figure sounds hard to believe, over 40% of teachers were engaging with research in 2010?

PHILIPPA: Or with somebody else's.

AL: Uh, huh. What do you mean by engaging, they were reading it or ...?

PHILIPPA: Well they were reading it and trying it out, you've got to remember the GTCE had ... I think it was 19,000 teachers involved in the Teacher Learning Academy, all of them doing micro-enquiry.

Pause 1: Isn't that incredible? At the chalk-face: no less than 19,000 teachers involved with micro-enquiries. And at strategic levels too – we hear of a National Teacher Research Panel; School-Based Research Consortium; Best Practice Research Scholarships and Teacher Research Grants. But it is also worrying – all are consigned to the footnotes of history:

PHILIPPA: I mean people forget about this because the big chopper came down but ... and all of those were research ... were being trained by the GTCE to be research leads in their school. So ...

AL: So all this policy has happened before?

PHILIPPA: Yeah.

AL: What's the big chopper that came down?

PHILIPPA: Well, all of the national ... so the GTCE had a Teacher Researcher Policy, QCDA [Qualifications Curriculum Development Authority] and the Teacher Researcher Policy built into their Curriculum Development Networks. The TDA [Teacher Development Agency] had a Teacher Researcher policy. Now all of the national agencies had Teacher

Researcher policies and many of the local authorities did. But then the coalition comes in, closes down all the quangos overnight; so all of those nationally supported and funded schemes went – and we'd helped all of them build archives of teacher-research in the public domain. All of that was taken off the web and buried in a basement.

Pause 2: Teacher-research at the whim of government policy? 'A chequered past' is a kind interpretation. The advent of grass-root movements and organisations such as researchED, the Teacher Development Trust and the Chartered College of Teaching are to be welcomed – and supported. Likewise, the independence of charitable organisations such as CUREE, the Institute for Effective Education and the Education Endowment Foundation is a necessity:

AL: If you look at the big picture do you think compared to 20 years ago that research used by teachers has advanced, has gone backwards, about the same?

PHILIPPA: It's gone forward a lot and we are known worldwide. I mean a lot of my international work tells me we are known and understood as leading the field still. So, yeah, it's moved forward a long way. How much it's moved forward since 2010, I am not sure. I really am not sure. You were sceptical about that GTCE report but it's there for you to look at. I mean –

AL: No, I'm not being sceptical, I'm just … I'm expressing my own ignorance.

PHILIPPA: Surprise, yeah.

AL: I'd be in Scotland at that time, I wouldn't be so aware of it.

PHILIPPA: I mean up to 2010 the big problem was the amount and kind of research … when we did an analysis of how little education research was focused on pedagogy. It was tending to be focused on the sociology of research; or if it was to do with the learning process, it was to do with the curriculum, not to do with pedagogy. So they set up the Teaching and Learning Research Fund which was helpful and they … were required to have teachers sitting on the research panels, to create spaces for teachers to co-research with the research projects; and to definitely get a lot more research done. And there was a lot more qualitative research done about pedagogy. It wasn't quantitative scientific research, it was more qualitative, textual; and some of it was good and some of it was less good … But that created a lot of space for partnerships between researchers and schools and teachers that was really helpful.

Looking backward

It is clear from this professional conversation that recent decades have witnessed the arrival and subsequent disappearance of several initiatives with the aim of improving teacher-research. However, overall, matters are progressing in a forward direction and, with some justification, both Philippa Cordingley of CUREE and Kevan Collins of the EEF claim that England is 'world-leading' with respect to evidence-based practices and education research. CUREE, EEF, IEE, NFER, researchED, research schools, Teacher Development Trust – the scope and range of these organisations are testament to such a claim. What, though, of my native land?

Scotland could credibly lay claim to be 'world-leading' with regard to teacher-research when the Chartered Teacher Scheme was at its peak – but since its demise? Well, notably, 'underpinning the Standard for Career-Long Professional Learning (CLPL) are the core principles of

Table 9.1 Key areas – standard for career-long professional learning

Key Area	Professional Actions
Enquiry and Research	• develop and apply expertise, knowledge and understanding of research and impact on education; • develop and apply expertise, knowledge, understanding and skills to engage in practitioner enquiry to inform pedagogy, learning and subject knowledge; • lead and participate in collaborative practitioner enquiry.
Educational contexts and current debates in policy, education and practice	• understand and explore the contexts and complexity in which teachers operate and the dynamic and complex role(s) of professionals within the educational community; • actively consider and critically question the development(s) of policy in education; • develop culture where learners meaningfully participate in decisions related to their learning and school; • develop and apply political literacy and political insight in relation to professional practice, educational change and policy development.

Source: GTCS (2012:10)

practitioner enquiry' (GTCS, 2012: 4). This standard is an aspiration for experienced teachers and draws upon the Chartered Teacher Scheme which, itself, was influenced by Judyth Sachs's concept of the *transformative professional* (see previous chapter). The standard is not only aspirational but also ambitious – especially with regard to the above (see Table 9.1).

Looking forward

Really? Teachers critically questioning education policy? In the confined spaces of staffroom conversations – 'Yes.' More openly, at union meetings – 'Yes.' But, as a function of their jobs and with the approval of employers? Teachers applying political literacy and political insight? Is this not the unions' role? Are these CLPL standards ambitious and aspirational – or merely fanciful? Does Scottish education really wish to be stocked with transformative professionals?

Well, a good place to ascertain the extent to which this is taking place – or not – is Education Scotland. This is an executive agency of the Scottish Government that is tasked with improving the quality of Scotland's education system. It brought together the work and responsibilities of Her Majesty's Inspectorate of Education and Learning and Teaching Scotland – with the latter having been the main organisation for developing the Scottish curriculum. In December 2017, Gayle Gorman took up the reins of HMCI Scotland and CEO Education Scotland; and on 24 June 2019, I traversed the 20 or so miles from my home in Royal Deeside to meet up with her in the Aberdeen office:

AL: … So we're talking about the Scottish Attainment Challenge. Gayle, would you like to per- haps just tell me a wee bit more about it?

GAYLE: Yeah, so the Scottish Attainment Challenge is now into its fourth year and is the biggest in Scotland, in the whole infrastructure investment in education. You know,

£275,000,000 focused on closing the poverty-related attainment gap across the whole of Scotland. So it's quite a significant policy area, quite a significant commitment by the government in terms of public funding ... and what we've seen is the huge impact that's having. Just for me, one of the things was the change in vocabulary that we heard in schools and we continue to hear. So ... individual teachers; because it's all very well having head teachers and senior leaders talking about closing the poverty-related gap – or targeting young people who need more – but, actually, for me, the significant shift is the conversations that individual teachers are having where they're aware of exactly the young people who are in the greatest need. Where they have really thought about and reflected on the intervention or support programme that that young person or couple of young people might need. *And they're really talking about addressing adverse childhood experiences, addressing the social issues, community issues, family issues, it's not just about the classroom. That's the most significant change I think I've seen in a long while in education* [emphasis added]. So the individual classroom teachers addressing the issue, openly talking about it, tracking their pupils' performance and intervening; and the other thing is being brave enough to say when an intervention is not working.

Pause 3: Might this be the beginnings of political literacy and insight? Classroom teachers freely addressing family, community and societal issues. And how might this be achieved?

AL: Okay, could you maybe give me an example of an intervention that works?

GAYLE: Yeah, so I mean there are lots ... but some of the things we've seen that have really shifted has been schools appointing Community Development Advisors, or Parent Outreach Workers ... who are working on Parent Support Programmes that are about the whole family, that are about ensuring we've created the conditions for a child to learn. So like in Renfrewshire, I'm sure when you spoke to Steven he might have mentioned this; they did the Pizza Maths Club, so they all come along for pizza, they're doing maths activities and it's a way of engaging with the whole family. Those we've seen are having a significant impact ...

AL: ... I mean some people might say, 'Well, that's not a school's job. You know, it's not the schools that cause these social problems ... we didn't cause it yet you expect us to fix it.'

GAYLE: Well, I think everyone has got to fix it. I think that's a valid point; I think everyone has got to fix it but, actually, if we really are, as a country, to address the poverty-related attainment gap then the schools can't do it alone. Absolutely can't. However, what they can't do is be isolated – because children live in families, live in homes, live in communities – and so, actually, the more interaction and interplay there can be between them – it actually strengthens the child's and young person's opportunity to learn and creates the conditions for them to learn. Because we know that working in partnership with parents and community is a great accelerator for children's progress.

AL: So, you're quite happy for the money to be spent on a community project that's maybe obliquely related to the school; but it helps the community?

GAYLE: As long as the school have looked at 'Is this going to work for our young people? Is this going to work for our community? How are we going to measure the impact? How are we going to evaluate?' ... And they are confident that decision should really be made by the school and the practitioners nearest the child who ... I could say, 'I think that would work; but I don't know that young person or that family – they do.'

AL: So the decision is made closest to the –

GAYLE: Closest to the child. Definitely!

Pause 4: The HMCI is indicating that there is a devolution of both finance and responsibility to the school with a clear acknowledgement that schools better understand their communities. This assertion is challenged, though, by the headline emblazoned across the front page of the 1 November 2019 edition of *The Herald* namely, *£200m 'shambles': questions grow over fund to help poorest children*. The writer, Williams (2019) cites evidence of unclaimed monies and a majority of teachers surveyed (n = 550) reporting that there is 'little or no evidence of impact'. Tellingly, there is an observation from the education spokesperson of Scottish Labour, Iain Gray, a former maths and physics teacher that: 'Targeted additional funding to raise attainment, especially literacy and numeracy amongst children from deprived families, is a good thing, albeit not new. Forty years ago when I was a teacher schools received extra funding to that end' (Williams, 2019).

More positively, the HMCI speaks of a 'reaching out' to communities such as we have already witnessed through Chris Wilson, HT Ramsden (Chapter 5) and the three Rotterdam schools (Chapter 6). There is no longer a dividing wall at the school gate – schools live in and for their communities – and the complexities of deprivation require collaboration:

AL: Okay. So collaboration is a big theme then, is it?

GAYLE: A huge theme. It's our biggest focus of Scottish education in terms of how we get from 'good to great' – and it's really important that individual practitioners collaborate. That we're allowing people to look in the school and collaborate ... because even nowadays we still go into schools where there's not a lot of collaboration within one school. Outside school with other schools, and you know even wider across the nation and internationally; and we have a job to play to make sure we support teachers to be able to access some of that evidence, that learning, that traditionally has been locked in individual institutions or local authorities.

AL: So at a school level, how does that work then, how does a teacher get funding or access to different schools?

GAYLE: So one of the things, the big policy changes there have been in the last sort of two years has been the 'empowerment agenda' – and so there was an education bill consulted on by the Scottish Government that had its core principles about collaboration, about evidence-based practice, about research ... and that a joint agreement had been reached between local government and national government. And I chaired the delivery body of that between unions, professional associations, parents, carers, everybody; the 'great and good' of Scottish education – and part of it was to put together packages and guidance that would allow teachers to feel confident in doing that. So, create the conditions for collaboration ... and the conditions for empowerment and we launched some of that Head Teacher Charter back in January; and we've released further guidance and materials by the end of August.

So, there's a huge shift around decision making and making people feel that they should ... I'm always talking to the profession about 'It's the profession taking back the profession'. And for a whole host of reasons, you know, people have sought permission either from their faculty head, from a principal teacher, from their head teacher, they've sought permission then from the local authority or ... and actually what we're trying to say is, 'When you know the learners, you make the right decision and you use your professional judgement; you learn from others to take that forward.' So, we've got things like there's grants for individual research programmes, there's grants for people to go on training, there's all of the Leadership Development Programmes ... two weeks ago, now, there was the release of the Career Pathway group outlining ten recommendations. So that, actually, you don't have to just think about institutional leadership anymore. If you want to lead pedagogy or lead a subject area, in Scotland that will be just as valuable as it is to become the leader in a school/head teacher. So, taking a Singapore type model, within a Scottish context; so that we're creating conditions, freeing up the system, getting rid of some of the red tape that there's been there and publicising that collectively as national, local and regional groups.

We've also got the Regional Improvement Collaboratives - so there are six areas across Scotland who've come together to support ... the whole purpose is to support collaboration and sharing; and to get networks of practitioners together to share ... If you're the geography expert and you're the only one in the secondary school these days you will have access to colleagues. You might have had a little group in your local authority but some of Scotland's local authorities are quite small; and so across a Regional Improvement Collaborative they can now network, they can get together; and we're seeing this kind of organic growth of some of those groups developing.

Pause 5: Another note of caution. These are aspirations, plans, albeit already showing signs of growth. But history reveals some sobering lessons.

Research grants - these were tried and tested by the General Teaching Council Scotland and are still available from the Educational Institute of Scotland: but uptake by teachers?

Leading pedagogy in schools - for decades, principal teachers (PTs) led pedagogy across Scotland's secondary schools - but these posts have largely disappeared. The Scottish Government and local authorities have created some of the gaps that they now seek to fill.

And, of course, the ill-fated Chartered Teacher Scheme (see Chapter 1) - this, too, had the approval and support of the 'great and the good' in Scottish education before its ultimate disappearance.

However, the Regional Improvement Collaboratives? This may be different. Perhaps this offers some of the benefits of England's Multi-Academy Trusts in which like-minded teachers work together for a common purpose (again, see Chapter 1). Indeed, maybe some of the 'outstanding work' identified by Education Scotland in West Dunbartonshire, Renfrewshire and Glasgow may become prevalent across the country. This would seem to be the intention by Education Scotland (2019: 8) when it reports upon the five key features that are evident in those challenge authorities making the greatest progress i.e.:

- Shared and embedded vision and values leading to a culture of relentless drive for improvement.
- Shared responsibility and leadership at all levels.
- High levels of expertise in data analysis to drive clear and outcome-focused self-evaluation.

- High-quality professional learning informed by self-evaluation, leading to improved learning and teaching.
- Very effective partnership working.

These five key features resonate widely – furth of the border with the East Midlands' work of The Forge Trust and the Ad Astra Primary Partnership (Chapters 1 and 3); the research-focused schools of South Yorkshire and Nottinghamshire (Chapters 4 and 5); the Research School of the Lincolnshire fens (Chapter 7); and thence to the edge of the European continent (Chapter 6):

AL: ... how long have they been going for, the Regional Improvement Collaboratives?

GAYLE: Two years. One of them has been going about six years, the one up here in fact, Northern Alliance. So, they've made rapid progress in that time, really, from a standing start some of them ... so the RICS [Regional Improvement Collaboratives] are places ... where people can come together in a group that they want to. If I think about some of the work that's going on not far from here; there's a huge Emerging Literacy pro-gramme that's been going on with Early Years Practitioners in Primary 1 and 2. That's a programme that started with some research, multi-agency; so speech and language therapist, Ed Psychologists, teachers sharing their expertise, developing an approach; and now that's from Shetland down to Argyll and Bute; and all around the whole of eight local authorities and involves hundreds of practitioners. That is about an organic growth and people upskilling themselves.

[...]

AL: That's what I'm trying to get to, is actually the spill over; people saying 'Well, we're doing these things here, they're really working, you might want to find out about it, we'll share it with you.'

GAYLE: That's exactly what's happening, so particularly ... authorities who've tried out some innovative practice or done different things; they're now through the Regional Improvement Collaboratives cascading that, and networking it, and people are saying, 'Okay, well I'm going to go back and do it this way...' ...

AL: Uh huh. Yeah, I've always looked at it that if something works somewhere else, it's only a working hypothesis.

GAYLE: Exactly!

AL: It may or may not work in your area.

[...]

GAYLE: ... I think you can have a coherent conversation across Scotland because of its size and scale. Actually, what's fundamental is what would work in Hazlehead Academy (Aberdeen) probably wouldn't work in Holy Cross in Glasgow; and we have to recognise that; and I think there's a growing understanding of that. It's more about challenge questions: how would you use that information? How do you evaluate where you are as a school ...?

... So, I think it's about creating the conditions where the information and research is available and easy for teachers who are really busy. We need to get much better at getting that information, and getting the evidence of what works well, out there: so that people can then reflect on it and use what's applicable to them but ... much more in a bespoke way.

AL: And do you have any plans for that...?

[...]

GAYLE: ... but we've also in the new Education Scotland, we've got a dissemination strategy about research and about effective practice in Scotland. Because one of the things we're not very good at is, like if a school gets a brilliant inspection report, usually locally, you hear about it. Well, actually, what we weren't very good at was actually telling the whole country about that. And so, we've had a head teacher come and join us. We go out and do interviews and discussions and gathering information with the schools involved; and then we turn it into a sketch note with related videos and research papers and different things; and we put it back out in the system.

AL: Under what heading?

GAYLE: Sketch notes.

AL: So I would find this on –

GAYLE: Go 'Education Scotland sketch notes' or look on Twitter, the Education Scotland Twitter page – we retweet them ... There's one-to-ones with the teacher, the practitioner, a parent, whoever; there's some paperwork behind it as well; and now there's a little thing on the visual called the Teachers Bookshelf where the research that the school used to make that ...base that improve[ment] on, is there.

AL: If I was in a school in Aberdeen and I got interested in what you've just talked about; would I know to go and look at sketch notes?

GAYLE: A lot of schools would; I mean we only started them this year but we were aiming to have about 6 out this year; and actually we're going to have about 25. So it's been great, it's been fantastic and schools have loved them. So social media, we use an awful lot now and actually it's got our biggest hits on anything we've done –

AL: Sketch notes? [See Figure 9.1.]

GAYLE: Sketch notes, hugely popular ... And actually we're kind of validating it; we're gathering the evidence so they don't have to spend the time. We're basing it around validated inspection findings.[4] We're able to say, 'No, you must talk about this because it's sector leading'. It's fantastic and building people's confidence and now we're actually seeing a few schools doing their own which is great ... So, it's becoming part of the narrative really quite quickly; and I think it's because people can quickly access the material but then also go deeper if they want, what lies behind it?

As our professional conversation drew to a close, I invited Gayle to reflect upon her experiences on both sides of the border:

AL: Okay and to finish ... would you like to compare your experiences of Scotland and England with regard to poverty. Because my experience would be that England is so much more fragmented; but it's quite dynamic. There's lots of different things happening there but now, coming back to Scotland, it's almost like in the short time I've been away, Scotland has become much more dynamic. What's your perception?

GAYLE: Pretty similar ... So, actually what I've seen in the last few years is this shift to a very dynamic system where there is a lot more creativity and people are encouraging each other in that creativity which is fantastic. I mean, it was always there but I suppose it's more apparent now. There's a lot more energy to it and some of that, I think, is related

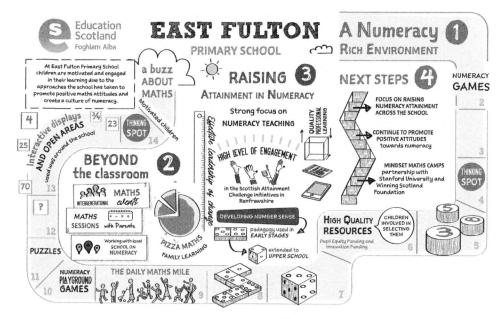

Figure 9.1 Sketch note – example
Source: https://education.gov.scot/improvement/documents/nih086-east-fulton-primary-school-sketchnote.pdf

to … giving that money directly to schools. [This] was a first in Scotland and people then reflected on this decision. It wasn't they weren't reflecting before but, somehow, because it was your money that the school had it seemed to have more of those conversations about teaching and learning and about pedagogical approaches – and that seems to have been a real fast track to then, this energy and capacity that we see in the system now, that is very dynamic and individual. And we're seeing more and more of that; and we're trying to create the conditions to see even more as we go forward.

AL: And you're not worried it might go right out of control, lots of things happening in places you'd never find out about?

GAYLE: Isn't that about making a decision nearest to the learner? I'm sure other people, maybe other politicians and various people may be concerned; but I'm an educator. I'm a teacher and actually I know this will have an impact. I wanted to make the decision for my children and my young people and so does every educator. So as long as people are keeping children at the heart of the decision making and reflecting on 'What's the outcome I want?' 'I want to improve their maths, I want to improve their capacity, I want to improve their confidence, whatever it happens to be.' And they're thinking about that and self-regulating; and making sure that they're having an impact – then, actually, that diversity should be a strength of the system and not a weakness. It's a strength that, actually, the approach in one school here would be very different to the one across the road, or one classroom, depending on the children and young people.

AL: It seems to me this Her Majesty's Chief Inspectorate isn't what it used to be?

GAYLE: We are very much the champions of Scottish education … So, we will absolutely be very clear about making sure children are getting the best deal – because they only get one chance – so we will very much do that. But what we're also doing is supporting the profession and representing the profession to build capacity and confidence within and across our system. Because we do see, as HMI, we do see the excellent practice that there is in Scotland. Okay, we sometimes see things that need to improve; but, actually, the good stories far outweigh anything else – and we want to give people the confidence to understand that in a system that's changing.

From my perspective, the professional conversation with Gayle Gorman, CEO of Education Scotland was refreshing and, to be honest, something of a surprise. I pay her the ultimate compliment – when Gayle says 'but I'm an educator. I'm a teacher' it is convincing. Gayle exudes enthusiasm and passion for teachers, for schools, for students and pupils. Albeit, it is a passion tempered by practicalities, realities, day-to-day challenges and obstacles: it is nonetheless real. However, a nagging doubt remains – what do classroom teachers think?

It is, of course, not possible to survey the attitudes of all Scotland's teachers; but there is a shortcut. The union. The EIS – the Educational Institute of Scotland. There are other fine trade unions such as the Scottish Secondary Teachers Association (https://ssta.org.uk) but with more than 80% of teachers within their ranks, the EIS stands foremost. Indeed, throughout my career, whenever a new initiative was mooted, or a major event was on the horizon, my colleagues often remarked, 'What does the union say?' And so, for my final professional conversation, I determined to find out what the union does have to say.

Notes

1 In 1967 the Celtic football team, comprising 11 players born within a 30-mile radius of Glasgow, were immortalised as the 'Lisbon Lions' when they became the first British team to win the European Champions' Cup with a 2-1 victory over Inter Milan in the Stadium of Light, Lisbon.
2 The mid-point sum of £55 million is worth approx. £105 million in 2020.
3 Shortly thereafter, further critical reports about educational research were commissioned by the Department for Education and Employment (the Hillage Report, 1998) and the Office for Standards in Education (Tooley and Darby, 1998).
4 This concept of 'validated inspection findings' is based upon an earlier comment from the HMCI namely, 'so we worked together as a system obviously. Education Scotland we had Audit Scotland as well because of the finance that's involved, it's significant. But we also had our peer assessors we called them for the first time. So people from other local authorities in similar positions, you know QIOs (Quality Improvement Officers) or Heads of Service, working as part of the inspection team alongside the local authority members themselves.'

References

Education Scotland. 2019. [Online] *How well are the Scottish Attainment Challenge authorities improving learning, raising attainment and closing the poverty-related attainment gap? Summary report.* June 2019. Available from: https://education.gov.scot/Documents/SACSummaryReport.pdf [Accessed 1 November 2019]

GTCS (General Teaching Council Scotland). 2012. [Online] *The Standard for Career-Long Professional Learning: supporting the development of teacher professional learning.* December 2012. Available from: www.gtcs.org.uk/web/FILES/the-standards/standard-for-career-long-professional-learning-1212.pdf [Accessed 1 August 2019]

Hammersley, M. 1997. Educational research and teaching: a response to David Hargreaves' TTA lecture. *British Educational Research Journal* 23(2) 141-161.

Hargreaves, D. H. 1996. [Online] *Teaching as a research-based profession:possibilities and prospects*. The Teacher Training Agency Annual Lecture 1996, pp. 1-12. Available from: https://eppi.ioe.ac.uk/cms/Portals/0/PDF%20reviews%20and%20summaries/TTA%20Hargreaves%20lecture.pdf   [Accessed 31 October 2019]

Hillage Report. 1998. *Excellence in research on schools*. University of Sussex: Institute for Employment Studies.

Tooley, J. and Darby, D. 1998. *Educational Research:A Critique*. London: Ofsted.

Williams, M. 2019. £200m 'shambles': questions grow over fund to help poorest children. *The Herald*. 1 November 2019, p.1.

10 Conversation in union

The Educational Institute of Scotland (EIS) is the world's oldest teaching union; founded in 1847. It has a concern for professional learning and collaborates with other interested parties in this provision; and it even sponsors action research projects. Notably, and very recently, it has combined with the Scottish Government to deliver professional learning on a national scale:

> PACT will design and deliver strongly research-based professional learning opportunities for all teachers and headteachers focused on school policy, practice and pedagogy that is rooted in social justice principles ... to minimise the damage that poverty and socio-economic disadvantage do to the education and life-chances of too many of Scotland's children.

> (www.eis.org.uk/Professional-Learning/PACT)

From a previous conversation, I was aware that the EIS General Secretary, Larry Flanagan, has a positive view of practitioner enquiry with which he had participated whilst principal teacher of English at Hillhead High School, Glasgow. He was instrumental in supporting the PACT initiative and thus, securing myself an invitation, on 26 August 2019, I proceeded to the Georgian New Town of Edinburgh – a World Heritage site and the location of the EIS headquarters:

AL: So, for once on my journey, it's a nice sunny day. I'm here in Edinburgh with Larry Flanagan and I bumped into a colleague of his who was mentioning a project called PACT – would you maybe, like to tell us a wee bit about it Larry?

LARRY: Yeah sure. PACT is a joint EIS Scottish Government project which is looking to develop capacity around teachers and schools addressing the impact of poverty on attainment. Its background is that for the last few years both the Scottish Government and the EIS have attended the International Summit on the Teaching Profession which is a kind of unique platform – because it's 50% government delegation, 50% trade union delegation and one cannot attend without the other ... (the) Scottish Government took up the UK place ... and myself and Mike Russell attended the summit. One of the things that happens at the summit is that in the last session ... you have to have a meeting within your delegation and agree three action points for your system for the next year. So, one of the action points that we had looked at was addressing the impact of poverty on educational attainment; and over the course of two or three years we developed joint approaches around that. So ... what is now Scottish Government policy, came a fair bit from these discussions...

AL: So, is this like where the Scottish Attainment Challenge came from; is this the background to it?

LARRY: No, it was in the background to it. I would'nae say it led directly to that; but it did lead through various iterations to us saying, 'One of the things you should do is use the expertise of teachers to talk to other teachers.' So two years ago we had agreed that we would develop a project which was designed to develop teacher capacity, school capacity to tackle the impact of poverty. We submitted a bid, and the Scottish Government is funding the project for ... I think it's three years is the initial funding. We appointed two workers; we have a board which involves Education Scotland, all the usual partners, the universities. What the two key workers are doing, one of whom was from a teaching background and one of whom was from working in the anti-poverty, third sector, is that they're looking to develop bespoke programmes for teacher training essentially. So, potentially, going in to do a post-school one-hour briefing on some of the issues around poverty or to do a full day's in-service. The model we're developing is to have various packages that can be used ...

It's the idea of creating in each area you work a cohort of champions who then take on further work ... So, it's about building a capacity at a school level.

AL: And is EIS supportive of that?

LARRY: Oh yeah –

AL: These champions in schools?

LARRY: Yeah we're ... in the early stages. We're looking at using our Learning Rep Network and our Equality Rep Network as obvious people to be part of the delivery. We've had fairly good buy in, in terms of the approach from the local authorities as well. So, if we were doing it in Glasgow we would expect people would get time out of school to go and deliver to another school; or you might do it on a cluster basis ... they're still building the partnership arrangements but we are pretty clear that when we get to the point of actually delivering, we want this to be EIS badged; so that it is people who are actually in classrooms who are coming out to talk to other people who are in classrooms – rather than being an external source. It's that idea that we discussed at the ... International Summit on the Teaching Profession ... It ticked our box, ticked the Scottish Government's box ...

AL: And how is that going to impact upon EIS financially in the future if you're going to have these clusters and local networks of expertise ...?

LARRY: No, we already run a more extensive CPD programme than people would probably anticipate. So, we do a lot of work already, much of it funded through the Scottish Union Learning Funding. So we run digital courses, ASN [Additional Special Needs] courses and they're always sold out. And we also run a lot of our own professional development, usually in partnership with somebody. We've done Glasgow Uni, Edinburgh Uni. Now at the moment we provide all of this; we don't charge members for taking part in any kind of CPD activity. But there are teacher trade unions across Europe where this is actually almost a kind of parallel stream to their work as a trade union, that they're a CPD provider. And they use the expertise of their members to deliver the CPD, there are different models in place. In the Netherlands, they have a whole system which is essentially retired teachers and they are the main CPD provider in their system. So –

AL: So it could be an income stream then?

LARRY: I've got to say, I don't think this was their intention but it certainly brings in more than they spend on it ... And we just think we can provide a good programme because, as I say, it's back to teachers talking to teachers and the PACT stuff builds on the Anti-Poverty Campaign that's been running for the last 4–5 years. Our Anti-Poverty Campaign has issued 'Tackling the Impact of Child Poverty' to schools, giving advice out to schools on 'Here are actions you can take now to address the impact of poverty'. Some of it predicated on the fact that because in some communities, poverty has been so endemic that there's a danger that you don't even realise it's something that has to be tackled. You just assume it's a given. I mean, back in the 1980s when I was a councillor in Glasgow, you had things the old Strathclyde Region called the Areas of Priority Treatment. I guarantee you go to almost any of these areas today and they're still the hotspot in terms of poverty. The East End of Glasgow, Shettleston, it's always been the same; so the cycle of poverty has'nae really been broken. And if you're working in that area then you might just think this is normal and not something that should have the extra attention paid to it.

[...]

So, I taught in Hillhead which is in the West End of Glasgow. Because it's next to Glasgow Uni people think 'Oh, that must be a good school, an affluent school.' We had 33% free meal entitlement because we took in Anderston, the city centre; we had loads of kids from Possil because it was on the bus route, loads of kids from Govan because it was on the subway.[1] When I was at the school its 33% free meal entitlement in almost any city in Scotland would get you additional resources, priority treatment. In Glasgow the threshold was 35% right, so one in three of your kids on free meals –

AL: Wasn't enough.

LARRY: Was'nae enough because, well, that's just the average, so we didn't get additionality in terms of staffing or resources.

AL: See the poverty though, I mean ... articles from like of Joan Mowat and the current edition of *Teaching Scotland*, talking about how complex it is, and it's got to be different organisations working together. I saw a good example of that in the Midlands – Sherwood Forest Education Partnership – where the folk from the libraries, the local health centre, worked with the local school and they're all collaborating together to address poverty and sharing information. So the library would find out what the school was doing, the school would find out from a client what's happening and it really was ... it was a grassroots approach. It was a multi-partnership approach ...

LARRY: That kind of partnership approach is the philosophy of the project. I suppose one of the differences is the role of the local authority because in England the local authority by and large is disconnected from schools now because of the whole academy programme and –

AL: In this one they were involved; the council was very involved.

LARRY: Uh huh. I mean, I think most people in Scotland would say it's accepted now that schools can't tackle the impact of poverty on their own and you do need a joined up approach [...] So, I think your point about the joined up approach and having different agencies and different groups involved in a strategy is critical ...

AL: ... Is there a kind of sea change taking place? In a sense, I feel like the time I spent in Lincoln, I had my back turned on the Scottish education scene; and I'm doing all this poverty stuff and I just kind of turned around – and then the Scottish Attainment Challenge was everywhere. Because, in the TES, you got the great report for Renfrewshire, and the great report for Glasgow. It looks really good; and I went to talk to Steven Quinn at Paisley ... about the collaboration and what they're doing. And I read a wee bit about your trip, saying that ... who's the writer on the TES that's been for years? He's ... he said that they're all –

LARRY: Hepburn!

AL: Hepburn, aye. He said it's like they're all singing from the same hymn sheet now. I mean, do you feel ... that inequality really is getting tackled now – or there has been a change in how we address poverty in schools?

LARRY: I think there's ... I made this point on a few platforms, there is now a really strong consensus across ... leave aside the party politics ... there's a really strong consensus that the single biggest issue is 'address the impact of poverty'. Now there's a whole debate beyond that about why have we still got poverty? ... If your school is'nae able to demonstrate, at least on paper, that it's mindful of the impact of poverty and it's doing something about it – you're going to get jumped on by HMI, your councillors, your Director of Education. So I think the fact that the system is almost singularly focused on addressing the impact of poverty is a sea change and even ... the political debate is about how effective the SNP [Scottish National Party] are in tackling it, or how ineffective they are. Even the Tories don't suggest that the issue is irrelevant.

AL: I kind of feel, though, that whoever came into power, if it was somebody else, they couldn't drop it. That's how I perceive it. You wouldn't be allowed to drop this, it's so high profile now. You might have a different take on it, or a different way of doing it, but you wouldn't be allowed to just park it to the side.

LARRY: No, that's right, you absolutely wouldn't – and when the SNP made it a priority, in one sense, they created a rod for their own back ... [but] since John Swinney coming in,[2] it's been a bit more couched in terms of we need to have a societal approach to it. But the only political debate beyond that is just how effective you've been in tackling it; because nobody was going to disagree about it being an issue. And that's partly because, unfortunately, poverty is so widespread across the whole of the country. Unless you represent only affluent areas, every political representative is going to be addressing the impact of poverty at some level. Even the impact of rural poverty, which was often underplayed, is now much better understood and a much stronger focus on it. Just because you live in what people might regard as a desirable geography does'nae mean that there is'nae poverty. So the –

AL: I got first told about that when I went to Aboyne Academy (Aberdeenshire) in 1991. I remember the deputy head, Mario de Maio, quite angry about it – they used the term rural poverty. He said, 'people don't realise there are kids who are living in little huts and cottages on somebody's big estate ...'

LARRY: Aye. So that focus, I think, is very welcome; and we spent a good few years always having to say schools cannae do it alone. Because Nicola Sturgeon said, 'judge me on education and closing the attainment gap' - it became the be all and end all. That was unfortunate; because if you really wanted to get a collaborative approach around addressing the impact of poverty - that can be nuanced much better. Closing the attainment gap isn't the only yardstick that should be used about what we're doing in terms of addressing the impact of poverty - because the attainment gap ... depending where you apply it, it nearly always ends up having a focus on the SQA stuff[3] and how many kids from poor backgrounds get to university ... If you say, 'Getting to university isn't the be all and end all', people go 'no, absolutely of course it's not!' Then you say, 'Well, why do you keep talking about it as if it is? You never talk about anything else.' So, some of that is a reflection of the political tensions around the debate. One of the things I think is irrefutable is that actually our ... kids in Scottish schools are more confident, more articulate, and I think more content than even 30 odd years ago when I started teaching.

AL: I mean, do you actually see that when you go back to Hillhead for that week you spend there, do you feel that's ... you've seen that with your own eyes?

LARRY: Yeah. I think on any school visits I do; I find the level of confidence that young people have got now - and their ability to articulate their own thoughts and feelings - is night and day from when I started teaching ...

AL: ... I remember doing my first [secondary] teaching practice, it was Fernhill which is adjacent to Castlemilk and the kids -

LARRY: I was a Castlemilk councillor.[4]

AL: Were you? And the kids -

LARRY: The other side of the wall.

AL: A hole in the wall. Aye, where they sniffed the glue in the crisp bags ... but the kids appreciated the order and the structure and the safety they got in school. They didn't give you problems ... you took them for football and things like that. They really enjoyed that.

LARRY: No, I think that's ... there's a huge amount of truth in that. Unfortunately, for some kids, school is their safe haven. Especially ... it's related to poverty but, especially, some family circumstances are more distressing than others. You know ... I did ... over a period of probably about five years, acting depute [head], I kept going back to my PT [principal teacher] post because I did'nae like it -

AL: Is this at Hillhead?

LARRY: Aye. I did it twice and did'nae apply for the job. One of the things as the depute, you dealt more one-to-one with some of the kids with issues; and you had access to their backgrounds in a way you did'nae get as a classroom teacher. So Pastoral Care might come in and say, 'So and so has had a difficult weekend, cut them a wee bit of slack.' But, actually, when you were seeing some of the detail of what was going on in the kids' lives -

AL: Pretty shocking.

LARRY: These kids are ... you got a referral from a teacher moaning about the way they're holding their pencil and you're thinking, 'Given their circumstances these kids are actually doing brilliant to be here.'

AL: You're saying exactly the same that Brian Wood, who was the head teacher at Hazlehead Academy in Aberdeen, said to me when I was talking to him. Just what you said; it was the teacher's lack of knowledge of the children's personal circumstances that annoyed them – because they were doing the very same thing you've just said – getting upset about some little minor thing because it was contradicting the classroom rules when, in fact, that child's background was horrendous. And he was saying, 'It was wonderful the kid's actually in school and is reasonably dressed.' That in itself is an achievement but the teacher didn't … doesn't know that …

LARRY: And also … issues of confidentiality do come into it. But coming back to the PACT project. One of the things about raising awareness of the impact of poverty and the consequences of poverty is that, thankfully, most teachers don't come from impoverished backgrounds. But the consequence of that is they won't necessarily know just how horrific it can be. If you and I missed our lunch we'd be like, 'I'm starving' by the time you get to eat. But you get kids coming into school without breakfast; it's not an experience that most people have gone through. Generally speaking, most teachers would have a summer holiday and be away abroad somewhere. You could'nae say that all the kids would have been. It was always … there was always an element of that. You come back and you tell the kids to write about your summer holiday –

AL: Well, there's a thing in the TES, 'don't do that'. Exactly the same, you ask them to write what they're going to do this year in school, don't talk about the holidays; because so many kids don't have holidays.

LARRY: That's right and –

AL: I never had holidays when I was younger and I come from a poor background, living in a tenement with an outside toilet you know so … I can understand that. A colleague, Elizabeth Farrar, was hitting on something you're saying about the disconnect between her middle class students:it's almost like they don't want to talk about poverty. It's almost like they can't mention the fact the kids are actually poor; as if it's insulting or offensive in some way. They don't really understand what poverty is about. So there obviously needs to be greater awareness of teachers of what it actually means for somebody to be poor; and to be able to talk about it.

LARRY: Yeah, I think the … I mean there were a lot … in the 1970s in particular, there were a lot more teachers who came from working class backgrounds – and you wouldn't necessarily be poor; but you'd probably know people that were poor. So … my dad worked in the shipyards, my mother worked in an office; so we were'nae poor – but you knew some of your pals that you played football with in the street, they had a harder time. So you were kind of aware that it was there but more and more teachers – the demographic will show you – they haven't come from poor backgrounds, that's not the norm for teachers. So, some of them have got very little experience of it. As you say … just not being aware of what poverty actually means. That example I gave you of the Queen's Cross Housing Association, the … you've got areas where both parents could be working or you could be a single parent working two or three jobs and they're only surviving. That has an impact as well. That's probably one of the areas where there's the least understanding because most people would tend to think, 'Well if you've got a job' –

AL: You're all right.

LARRY: You'll be all right. I got the bus into Glasgow last week and it was £5.50 for a day return and I'm going like that, £5.50!

AL: From where?

LARRY: From Renfrew into Glasgow.[5]

AL: Renfrew?

LARRY: Aye. So I'm like that's £5.50!

AL: And you're going like that.

LARRY: Aye. Because I don't get the bus that often; but I was leaving the car for some reason and I went –

AL: That's a lot of money.

LARRY: Imagine you're paying that every day to go to your work. You can get a five-day ticket or whatever but ... that would be a barrier right. And while you wanted to take your kids into the Science Centre, it's going to cost you twenty quid [£20] just to get on the bus and get back. So things that ... things that my kids took as read –

AL: They don't get that. That's a theme that's come up about the poverty of experience. Some of the schools actually, deliberately fund theatre trips because they know the kids aren't getting it. It's not going to happen in their home life; so we've got the money and we'll take it. But it's even spread to clinical things. The kids don't get eyesight tests anymore; so one of the head teachers, Chris Wilson, is actually employing on a part-time basis an optician. And he's got a wee place built in the school and that's almost like their own school clinic. Whether a school should be doing that or not, you can have a political debate about – but he's just addressing the need. He said, 'to read a book you need to have good eyesight, you need glasses, we'll provide it'.

LARRY: But that is where PEF money can help because –

AL: The Pupil Equity Fund?

LARRY: Aye. So ... some of the other areas, PEF may well be paying for that optician. Those are the areas where you think you need to know the school and the school community to be able to spend that money wisely. So in those areas, I think the PEF money is having an impact. I mean, I think all the money is having an impact ... whether it should have been there in the first place or whether PEF's real additionality is the debate. So ... the ... so there was new money announced with PEF; that £500 odd million that could have been in the grant settlement. Why was it not in the grant settlement? Well, because the Scottish Government did'nae trust local authorities to spend it on education. So, effectively, they ring-fenced it by saying we're giving it straight to schools.

AL: Well, just being personal, I think that's a good thing. Honestly, that that money is effectively ring-fenced and that's what it should be directed to.

LARRY: We've had a bit of a debate around it because we're obviously supporting local authorities in terms of the budget settlements. We ultimately said, 'if this is a way of ring-fencing it then we should just do it'. ... So ring-fencing is a practical issue for me, rather than a local democracy issue. Is it going to protect the money and get it spent in the way we want it spent? The other debate is about how much money is available but that's a different –

AL: Different discussion ... So, is there anything you want to finish with Larry ...?

LARRY: I think our schools are better communities than they were; and I think we've made a lot of progress in terms of ... you talk about young people's resilience and so forth; but just basically, you know, they're happy in school and they enjoy their learning by and large. So making sure we capture that and that we nurture it, is as big a prize, as closing the attainment gap ...

Conclusion

There is much upon which to ponder regarding this extract from the professional conversation with Larry Flanagan e.g.:

- *Appropriate measures for determining the attainment gap.* For the most part, the measures used are quantitative and often relate to exam pass rates, percentages (e.g. students from deprived areas attending university) and numbers (e.g. free school meals). Less use is made of qualitative measures that are, of course, more time consuming and expensive to obtain.
- *Teachers' mobility and recruitment.* With regard to mobility, it is often discussed but little enacted that incentives should be in place in order to attract high-quality teachers to areas of socio-economic deprivation. But, if the role of a teacher is to 'make a difference' then is not the incentive sufficient that these are the areas where teachers make the greatest impact? In terms of recruitment; should there be recruitment quotas with universities and teaching schools being required to enrol a minimum percentage of students from working class backgrounds?
- *Teachers' understandings of poverty.* PACT and similar initiatives are important first steps in further raising the awareness of teachers with respect to poverty-related issues. But might not local authorities consider letting good quality accommodation, at minimal rents, to teachers in, or near to, areas of socio-economic deprivation?
- *The complexity of poverty, especially when it is deep-seated within a community requires community and inter-institutional responses.* My experience with the Sherwood Forest Education Partnership in Nottinghamshire provides a striking example of a community response. Likewise, the professional conversation with Sandra, head teacher at an inner-city Rotterdam school.
- *Funding streams and their applications to address poverty issues.* An ever present problem with diverse solutions; but the more finance and autonomy regarding decision making that is devolved to those with the greatest responsibility seems to be a fair response.
- *Relationships between national government, regional authorities and teaching unions.* There is a strategic role to be played with benefits clearly demonstrated by the Scottish Attainment Challenge. Perhaps Regional Improvement Collaboratives – or something similar – offers a model by which to harness national overview with the lived, day-to-day practicalities.

It is time now to draw this journey of closing the attainment gap in schools by making progress through evidence-based practices to a conclusion.

Notes

1 An underground metro system.
2 John Swinney is Deputy First Minister and Secretary for Education.
3 SQA is the Scottish Qualifications Authority responsible for the administration of national examinations.
4 At that time, Castlemilk was the largest housing estate in Europe.
5 The town centre of Renfrew is just over 9 miles from the city centre of Glasgow.

11 Collaboration for collective impact

Complexity and cultural responsiveness

Poverty is endemic: even Scripture bemoans that 'the poor you will always have with you' (Matthew 26:11). Larry Flanagan commented upon this saying that, today, it was the same areas in Glasgow suffering from economic deprivation as when he commenced his teaching career 40 years ago. Similarly, my return to the Vale of Leven was surprising in the relative lack of change it revealed since pounding the beat there in the 1970s. Indeed, there is widespread academic support that, broadly speaking, efforts to combat poverty have been largely unsuccessful. These observations support the argument of McKinney (2014: 203) that, 'Poverty, child poverty and the relationship with school education are serious issues for contemporary societies ... and present complex conceptual and methodological challenges that cannot be reduced to simple causes, effects and solutions.'[1] Within these pages this complexity is acknowledged by such as HMCI Scotland, the leader of Glasgow City Council and others. Such complexity prompts Mowat (2018: 299) to argue for a holistic approach to poverty rather than focusing narrowly upon attainment outcomes; and this approach should take cognisance of the socio-economic impacts upon families in poverty since, quite simply: '"Schools cannot go it alone": there is a need to focus upon a wide range of public policy to redress inequalities in society.'

Mowat's assertion firmly backs up the findings of the BERA (2016: 5) Research Commission on Poverty and Policy Advocacy that came 'to recognise that tackling child poverty through education alone is not possible [as] schools cannot compensate for society'. From a practitioner's perspective, this is corroborated by Alan Murray, former acting head teacher of Hazlehead Academy, Aberdeen when we met up for a professional conversation (Stonehaven, 30 May 2019): 'Schools don't cause the attainment gap; they provide a setting for it to be measured in the exam system. The attainment gap is caused by social factors, everyone knows that.' Speaking similarly, from an education perspective, Steven Quinn, above, points to the beginning of a solution to address poverty with his plea for a collective will emanating from classrooms, departments, schools and authorities across the nation.[2]

Affirmation from the States

Intriguingly, Steven Quinn's notion of 'collaborating for collective impact' finds support within the US education system where Tileston and Darling (2009) argue that:

> schools and teachers can create *culturally responsive* educational environments, based on collectivist value systems ... [in which] the role of the school leadership is crucial in the process of creating a *culturally responsive* classroom ensuring a high-quality education for all.
>
> (quoted in McKinney 2014:211, emphases in original)

This description of a culturally responsive educational environment is most apt for the work of the Ad Astra Primary Partnership, The Forge Trust, the Scottish Attainment Challenge and others discussed herein. The head teachers of the six Ad Astra schools identified the culture of their schools and local areas as being primarily 'White British Working Class in Areas of Underachievement'. Further, they identified particular features of this culture as being the five Perspectives of Poverty i.e. material, emotional, language, experience and aspiration. Their collective response was to create a high-quality education for all through addressing these five perspectives. This response enabled these schools to make progress in closing the attainment gap and examples of their evidence-based practices are to be found in the sections 'Mansfield Against poverty' and 'Amber Valley Against poverty' as discussed in Chapter 3.

Starting points and toolkits

Of course, if a school senior leadership team (SLT) is considering evidence-informed practices to combat poverty, then I would highly recommend that they engage with the work of Stoll et al. (2018) that is published online by the Chartered College of Teaching namely, *Evidence-informed teaching: self-assessment tool for schools*. This toolkit enables a SLT to 'evaluate and consider their own levels of interaction with evidence in terms of awareness, engagement and use' (Stoll et al., 2018:2). There are three indicators for a school to evaluate its own awareness of research evidence; six indicators for engagement i.e. drawing upon research evidence to inform and improve practice; and seven indicators to self-assess 'the degree to which research evidence is actively used to investigate and change practice' (Stoll et al., 2018:3). Across the 16 indicators the SLT are able to plot their progress from *starting out* to *deepening* then *embedding* (see Figure 11.1).

Such a systematic approach from a SLT should ensure that the school has a sound base upon which to raise awareness, engage and use research evidence. However, a SLT needs to take most, if not all, of their school colleagues with them on this journey. Drawing upon the work of Hayes et al. (2006), Lingard et al. (2003) and Wrigley et al. (2012), McKinney (2014:211) argues for productive schools that are imbued with:

> a leadership that shares the vision of the productive learning environment with teachers, children and young people and parents and facilitates or co-facilitates the conceptual, curricular and procedural changes to move towards productive pedagogies for the whole school. The leaders are able to share leadership ... with teachers.

Understanding what research evidence is, knowing how to access research, being able to objectively judge how robust research evidence is, knowing that it can help improve practice, how it does that, and how to go about being 'evidence-informed'.

Area of development. A1.

Head teachers and senior leaders understand evidence-informed teaching and what high-quality evidence looks like.

Starting out - Senior leaders are aware of some research evidence, but are not confident in how to judge the quality of research.

Deepening - Senior leaders are aware of some research evidence. They tend to do things because 'the research says' or rely on others' judgement to assess the quality of research. They do not necessarily engage critically with findings.

Embedding - Senior leaders are very aware of research evidence. They are able to judge its quality and to engage critically with findings. They also refer to trusted research sources e.g. EEF/Sutton Trust toolkit, John Hattie etc.

Figure 11.1 Awareness: school-wide
Source: Stoll et al. (2018: 4)

This appellation of 'productive schools' sits well with the Ad Astra Primary Partnership, The Forge Trust, Bawtry Mayflower primary school, Ramsden primary school and Rotterdam's Emmaus, Hildegardis and Maria schools. All of these schools have strong leaders - there can be little doubt of this. And all are, to varying degrees, visionaries. They are inspired by the possibilities that education makes available for their pupils. To different degrees, they question the role of schools being socially reproductive i.e. 'the process whereby a society reproduces itself over time and so maintains its identity across the generations' (Carr, 1993: 6). After all, the society in which their schools are sited is unjust - why should they aim to preserve the status quo and reproduce this kind of society?

Social production vs social reproduction

> They (schools) can serve ... as levers of social production. They can be in the vanguard of social change.
>
> (Hamilton 1990: 55)

Basically, schools can either be socially reproductive and accept society as it currently operates; or they can be socially productive and have the aim of changing society. Teachers tend to be conservative and sit more comfortably within the socially reproductive camp. Closing the attainment gap then becomes a series of exercises by which schools seek evidence-based practices that will help to narrow the gap for their pupils within the prevailing society. Perhaps, though, it is time to become *socially productive* and to 'be in the vanguard of social change'. This need not be as dramatic as it sounds.

Within Chapter 8 there is a discussion of early experiences with enterprise learning and the TVEI as mooted by Thatcher's second Conservative Government. Initially, this appeared to be a right-wing *putsch* by which the habits of *enterprise* were to become instilled within the world of education. However, unfounded fears of producing a nation of *Del Boys*[3] soon gave way to the realisation that enterprise learning was about harnessing and developing the talents of *all* of the pupils. At its best, enterprise learning promoted collaboration within the classroom such that all pupils worked *with* and *for* each other i.e. collaboration for collective impact.

Likewise, today, all political parties accept the need to address the poverty-related attainment gap and that this can only be achieved through a multi-agency approach. Again, there must be collaboration for collective impact. A single school (e.g. Ramsden near Worksop); a single Trust (e.g. Nottinghamshire's The Forge Trust); a single, local authority (e.g. Renfrewshire Council) – left to their own devices, each single entity will have a limited impact. However, in collaboration with other schools, other Trusts, other local authorities their collaborative impact will be greater. Additionally, it cannot be limited to education institutions – other agencies such as medical, library, psychological have a role to play. But who is to organise?

Given that we are speaking of a political vision of a socially productive society that harnesses and promotes the talents of all of the pupils – then government, of whatever political hue, has a central role to play: but it must be 'light touch', facilitative. As with the EIS-Scottish Government PACT initiative it must endeavour, initially, to raise the awareness of all teachers with regard to poverty-related issues. However, there needs to be a framework in which to operate; a source of expertise and support; and pedagogy – and these are the 'gifts' offered by England, Scotland and the Netherlands respectively.

England – research schools

Truly, with respect to evidence-informed and evidence-based practices then England is world-leading. There is a rich history of committees, strategies and interventions to promote action research and practitioner enquiry. Further, there is a plethora of institutions and organisations dedicated to the promotion of evidence-informed and evidence-based practices. Neither Scotland nor the Netherlands can hope to emulate this – nor should they. England has a critical mass of population that far exceeds these neighbouring countries i.e.:

- Estimated 2019 population of England – 66.43 million (http://worldpopulationreview. com/countries/england-population/)
- Estimated 2019 population of Netherlands – 17.10 million (http://worldpopulationreview. com/countries/netherlands-population/)
- Estimated 2019 population of Scotland – 5.25 million (http://worldpopulationreview.com/ countries/scotland-population/)

Rather, I should like to conclude by postulating one strategy or intervention or institution that each country can offer the others. *From England, I suggest research schools*. The reason for this is twofold. First, the experience of Bawtry Mayflower primary school. As discussed earlier, Bawtry had a degree of expertise with practitioner enquiry unrivalled by nearby schools. However, it acted in isolation. According to the head teacher, Julie Jenkinson, the local authority of Doncaster Metropolitan Borough Council paid little to no interest in their expertise: but the arrival of Doncaster Research School changed all of this. According to their website:

Doncaster Research School by Partners in Learning aims to lead the way in the use of evidence-based practice and bring research closer to schools. Through our existing networks we will share what we know about putting research into practice, and support schools to make better use of evidence to inform their teaching and learning so that they really make a difference in the classroom.

(https://researchschool.org.uk/doncaster/about/)

Clearly, they have harnessed the talents of Bawtry staff such as Julie Jenkinson and Claire Dunn, both of whom have leading roles within the Doncaster Research School. This sharing of expertise has enabled Bawtry staff to come into contact with a wider range of staff, many of whom work in schools sited in areas of socio-economic deprivation.

Second, my professional actions and conversations with James Siddle, Director of Lincoln's Kyra Research School. Whilst acknowledging that James is atypical with respect to his level of expertise, it is clear that research schools offer a locus in which teaching staff feel comfortable – and yet are challenged – to develop their knowledge and evidence-informed practices. Moreover, the introduction and development of associate research schools is to be welcomed as are the new research-based roles such as Evidence Leads in Education (ELEs). This English initiative from the Education Endowment Foundation and the Institute for Effective Education of creating research schools is worthy of consideration by the Dutch and Scottish governments. In order to close the attainment gap in schools through evidence-informed practices, it is not only necessary to have a secure knowledge base but also helpful to have expertise near-to-hand. At the time of writing, England has a network of 32 research schools + 7 associate schools. In terms of population for the Netherlands and Scotland this equates to eight and three schools respectively. The latter already has in place six Regional Improvement Collaboratives (RICs) that have been 'formed with the purpose of improving education and closing the poverty-related attainment gap in the schools in their areas' (https://connect.scot/news/regional-improvement-collaboratives-what-are-they). Further collaboration across the RICs could lead to the development of three research schools in order to enhance the collective impact.

Scotland – Regional Improvement Collaboratives

My *second suggestion* is that the Scottish provision of *Regional Improvement Collaboratives* is an initiative worthy of imitation by England and the Netherlands. At this regional level, it is possible to have oversight of initiatives such that different institutions and organisations may collaborate for collective impact e.g. the invaluable support and expertise offered by the West Dunbartonshire Psychological Service; the role of speech and language therapists for the Emerging Literacy programme within the Northern Alliance, etc. A RIC can provide an opportunity, a means by which to bring together a wide variety of expertise that is not usually available to a single department, or a single school, or a single authority.

England already has a skeletal framework in place with its Regional Commissioners (www.gov.uk/government/organisations/regional-schools-commissioners/about) and a national network of Teaching Schools Alliances (https://tscouncil.org.uk) some of which already have specific expertise regarding closing the attainment gap (e.g. see Lough, 2019). Moreover, if England and the Netherlands are to adopt the structural provision of RICs there should be a clear role for both the Dutch Inspectorate of Education (https://english.onderwijsinspectie.nl/inspection) and Ofsted. I only have to recall the excellent work undertaken by Peter Stonier (www.gov.uk/government/publications/ofsted-pen-portraits-of-her-majestys-inspectors-hmis/ofsted-hmi-pen-portraits) in his role as head teacher at Jacksdale primary school in the East Midlands to know that Ofsted has much to offer in this regard. Scotland's HMCI, Gayle Gorman, is a role model for what can be achieved by someone with that level of authority, expertise and enthusiasm.

Speaking of authority, expertise and enthusiasm ...

Netherlands - *Leerkracht*

The *third suggestion* derives from the spirit and practices of *Leerkracht* witnessed during the visit to Rotterdam. The three primary school head teachers - Anke, Judith and Sandra - have a wealth of experience in addressing the poverty gap and, indeed, their lives and practices are steeped in it. Strangely, they share similar flaws and strengths. They are flawed in that they are too quick to implement change - it should all happen yesterday. However, they have learned from their experiences of being a 'red Ferrari' as they now understand the need to take their teaching staff with them. Also, it is ok if some staff are steady and cautious since this can be a strength for the school - as it 'puts on the brakes' and gives all of the staff time to pause and reflect.

Most importantly, they have the collective wisdom to counter the 'steering paradox' whereby they empower their teachers to take control. The staff are encouraged to innovate, at their own pace, and to share their findings with each other. This approach may require further systemisation and rigour such as with the Disciplined Inquiry Approach but, ultimately, it should lead to Moore's (2012) idea of the teacher as practitioner + researcher + theorist. Moore's idea sums up my lifetime career - but my time has come and gone. Today, it is epitomised by the wonderful teachers whom I've met, such as Claire Dunn and Julia Crawshaw at Bawtry Mayflower and Sophie Longney *CTeach* (now Vice Principal) at The Sir Donald Bailey Academy, Newark. And there are so many others.

To cite but one example. I think of Katie Wilson, deputy head teacher at Eye Church of England primary school in Peterborough. During our professional conversation at her school (2 May 2019) she spoke eloquently of Rosenshine's principles of instruction, cognitive load theory and retrieval practice. Katie spoke engagingly about the influence of a mentor, Laura Wookey, now Lead Practitioner: Teaching and Learning with Nottingham-based Flying High Trust and who, in a previous post, had met with John Hattie in Australia such was her interest in research. And Katie spoke with refreshing honesty about the travails and joys of providing excellent CPD for teacher colleagues - often at no cost - sited within schools facing financial difficulties. As with Sophie Longney (see Chapter 8) she is an activist teaching professional 'who thinks critically, acts ethically and seeks justice'. Listen to her own words:

KATIE: I think a lot of it really comes from I suppose word of mouth ... and also because we've offered, so I've offered with ... initially with ... I think we put on like a grammar CPD session for the local authority and because people ... people thought, 'Oh, that sounds really interesting, can we find out more?' And I was like, 'Of course, come into the school, come and see it. Don't just take my word for it' – and schools did come in; and sometimes they came in several times to look at several different things ... then they came in again and it spread around, which is what you want, because ultimately that is what we are here for. We're here to make sure ... I think we've got that moral obligation to make sure that all schools and all pupils and all teachers have access to high-quality training, high-quality CPD and research that perhaps, sadly, not everyone in our profession does have the access to.

AL: Okay, so where does this moral drive come from then?

KATIE: I think the moral drive comes from working, I suppose in my career and the leaders here in schools where there has been high social deprivation and really tight budgets. And you know, we've wanted to ... a way around ... to tackle ... for not being to kind of, I suppose, afford to go on the fancy courses. We've had to go and investigate ourselves, I suppose, excellent practitioners. So, as a way of CPD, we've gone out to see other people in their classrooms and thought ... 'Ah, actually I can do this.'

For me, teachers such as Katie and Sophie are inspirational; and they are not alone. But their work requires to be nurtured, sustained and shared. Katie's work is known within her own school and those other schools that benefit from Eye's generous CPD provision. Sophie's work is known across The Forge Trust. But if their work were linked with a research school? If their work was shared across a Regional Improvement Collaborative? Then education may cease to have a sieve-like memory and there may be less need to re-invent the wheel. As Katie and Sophie amply demonstrate, *Leerkracht* is already to be found within this new breed of teachers for whom evidence-informed practices are intrinsically bound with research and theorising. These small groups of teachers in Bawtry, Eye and Newark – they exercise autonomy, reflect upon practices, innovate and share, seek out new ideas. As they collaborate for collective impact their work can both influence and be informed by research schools that, in their turn, will do likewise with Regional Improvement Collaboratives. If the teaching profession is to truly close the attainment gap in schools through evidence-informed practices, then it needs the *Leerkracht*. For it can only be through such collaboration for collective impact that a vision can be realised: and the vision is that of creating a society whereby the talents of *all* are realised:

> Where there is no vision, the people perish.
> (Proverbs 29:18)

Notes

1 Here McKinney draws upon the work of McKendrick (2011).
2 Quinn's assertion commands support from Mowat (2019: 64-65) who speaks of 'The purpose of this is to "unleash greatness" within the system by encouraging school leaders to work collaboratively together in partnership, transferring "knowledge, expertise and capacity within and between schools so that all schools improve and all children achieve their potential".'
3 Del Boy was a spiv-like character in the highly acclaimed television series *Only Fools and Horses*

References

BERA. 2016. *The Research Commission on Poverty and Policy Advocacy*. London: BERA.

Carr, W. 1993. Reconstructing the curriculum debate: an editorial introduction. *Curriculum Studies* 1(1) 5-9.

Hamilton, D. 1990. *Learning about Education: An Unfinished Curriculum*. Maidenhead: Open University Press.

Hayes, D., Mills, M., Christie, P. and Lingard, B. 2006. *Teachers and Schooling Making a Difference*. Sydney: Allen and Unwin.

Lingard, B., Hayes, D., Mills, M. and Christie, P. 2003. *Leading Learning: Making Hope Practical in Schools*. Maidenhead: Open University Press.

Lough, C. 2019. Ambition Institute appoints new chief executive. *Times Education Supplement*. 29 August 2019. Available from: www.tes.com/news/ambition-institute-appoints-new-chief-executive [Accessed 23 April 2020]

McKendrick, J. H. 2011. What is poverty? In J. H. McKendrick, G. Mooney, J. Dickie and P. Kelly (Eds) *Poverty in Scotland 2011*. London: Child Poverty Action Group, 17-29.

McKinney, S. 2014. The relationship of poverty to school education. *Improving Schools* 17(3) 203-216.

Moore, A. 2012. *Teaching and Learning: Pedagogy, Curriculum and Culture*. 2nd ed. Abingdon, Oxon: Routledge.

Mowat, J. G. 2018. Closing the attainment gap – a realistic proposition or an elusive pipe-dream? *Journal of Education Policy* 33(2) 299-321.

Mowat, J. G. 2019. 'Closing the gap': systems leadership is no leadership at all without a moral compass – a Scottish perspective. *School Leadership & Management* 39(1) 48-75.

Stoll, L., Greany, T., Coldwell, M., Higgins, C., Brown, C., Maxwell, B., Stiell, B., Willis, B. and Burns, H. 2018. [Online] *Evidence-informed teaching: self-assessment tool for schools*. Available from: https://chartered.college/wp-content/uploads/2018/01/Evidence-informed-teaching-self-assessment-tool-for-schools.pdf [Accessed 13 December 2019]

Tileston, D. W. and Darling, S. K. 2009. *Closing the Poverty and Culture Gap*. Thousand Oaks, CA: Corwin.

Wrigley, T., Thomson, P. and Lingard, B. 2012. Resources for changing schools: Ideas in and for practice. In T. Wrigley, P. Thomson and B. Lingard (Eds) *Changing Schools: Alternative Ways to Make a World of Difference*. Abingdon, Oxon: Routledge.

INDEX

Printed in Great Britain
by Amazon

37143043R00084